The Morris Canoe

Legacy of an American Family

Kathryn Hilliard Klos

Profits from the sale of this book support the mission of the Wooden Canoe Heritage Association, whose membership has kept the Morris canoe in use nearly a century after the factory ceased production, and whose interest in knowing more about these canoes and the men who built them has led to this writing.

Copyright © 2014 Kathryn Hilliard Klos
All rights reserved.
ISBN: 1492746916
ISBN-13: 978-149274691

Dedicated to the members

of the Wooden Canoe Heritage Association

--past and present--

who have kept alive

that which is

beautiful

finely built

and enormously fun to paddle—

whether or not it's a Morris

PADDLES UP!

Salute at WCHA Assembly 2014 (courtesy Jim Wilson)

Contents

Chapter 1	FROM FISH TO MORRIS	9
Chapter 2	A HOME IN VEAZIE	14
Chapter 3	OFF TO WAR	21
Chapter 4	THE CANOE BUILDERS ARRIVE	34
Chapter 5	BEGINNINGS	38
Chapter 6	THE INDIAN CANOE AND ITS DESCENDANTS	55
Chapter 7	ANATOMY OF A MORRIS CANOE	87
Chapter 8	THE CANOES OF BELLE ISLE	118
Chapter 9	THE VEAZIE CANOE COMPANY	136
Chapter 10	ENDINGS	148
Chapter 11	UP FROM THE ASHES	173

Chapter 12	DATING A MORRIS CANOE	181
Chapter 13	MORRIS MYSTERIES	199
EVENT TIMELINE		207
2014 MORRIS DATABASE STATISTICS		210
COMPANIES AND MATERIALS USED BY MORRIS		215
MORRIS "FUN FACTS"		244

Words from the Author

This book is not "a how-to" for the authentic restoration of the Morris canoe—there are several good books and other resources available regarding canoe restoration, and they are listed herein. However, I have included pictures and descriptions that demonstrate aspects of the Morris which may help the owner of a needy canoe understand what might be required to return it to what it once was.

Researching *The Morris Canoe* has been a treasure hunt that began with the purchase of a Morris in 2006. This journey is shared in notes following some of the chapters. As there is no better way to travel than by canoe, I have titled these notes "Paddle Strokes". Any of my informational sources can be found in this place, along with additional thoughts and images.

My research is on-going, as historical research has a tendency to unearth new questions while providing answers. New information will be shared on the website of the Wooden Canoe Heritage Association and in the journal *Wooden Canoe*. I welcome questions—and I especially welcome any new discoveries. Learning about one additional canoe can change what we believe we know about all of them.

The following are gratefully acknowledged for their contributions to the fulfillment of this project:

The Membership of the Wooden Canoe Heritage Association, past and present, for information shared either directly with me or through articles in *Wooden Canoe*; great-grandchildren of Charles Morris, Joyce Monforte, Louie King, and the late Ellen Waltz, for sharing family stories and pictures; Bob Topliff, for sharing the house he purchased from Morris family descendants and ephemera helpful to my research; Pete Metcalf of the Veazie Fire Department, for his discovery of the exact date of the Morris factory fire; Paul Miller, for pointing out that his Veazie canoe had only two pairs of cant ribs, thus providing an important clue; Howard Herman-Haase, for research conducted in a Harvard University Library that provided several answers and clues; historians in the towns of Veazie, Bangor, and Augusta, for responses to my research queries; Greg Nolan and Deborah Gardner, for permitting me use of their home in Dover-Foxcroft as a research base; my gracious readers and feedback-providers, Benson Gray, Dan Miller, Jerry Stelmok, Rollin Thurlow, Greg Nolan, Howard Herman-Haase, and Fred Campbell; my daughter Margaret Barnes, for creating the book's cover; and the late Denis Kallery, for setting my feet on this path in the first place.

--Kathy Klos

Denis and I paddle Dave McDaniel's *Virginia*

Kathryn Hilliard Klos

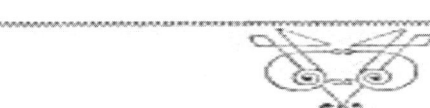

Cover of 1919 B.N. Morris Catalog surrounded by dingbats from the 1893 catalog, courtesy *The Historic Wood Canoe and Boat Manufacturer Catalog Collection* edited by Daniel Miller and Benson Gray

1

FROM FISH TO MORRIS

What's in a name? That which we call a rose by any other name would smell as sweet. – William Shakespeare

On April first of 1856, Albion Fish of Bangor, Maine, filed a petition on behalf of himself, his wife Sophronia and their three young children, changing their name from Fish to Morris. The name-change may have been suggested by Albion's father, Samuel Laine Fish, who lived in near-by Veazie, Maine; Samuel had changed his name to Morris ten days earlier. On that day, Samuel's half-brother Silas Fish of Leeds, along with his wife and children, also became Morrises. Altogether, the names of twenty members of the Fish family were changed, yet until March of 1856, the name "Morris" appears nowhere in the family's genealogical record.

While the seventy-three-year-old patriarch of the Fish family, Seth Fish, also changed his name to Morris on March 22, it seems he never used the name. The name he'd been accustomed to using for seventy-three years may have been comfortable-enough, and he decided to leave the use of this new name to those of his family-line who chose to do so. Despite this legal name-change, the name "Fish" would be inscribed on Seth's tombstone at his death four years later. His wife Abigail and their three minor children would also decline the use of

Morris, although their names had been legally changed. Perhaps the fact that most of Seth Fish's many children from two marriages retained the name of Fish weighed upon this decision.

The reason behind adoption of the Morris name by members of the Fish families of Leeds and Veazie has been lost to Time; however, the fact of it attached the name "Morris" to a brand of canoe that is valued today not only for its beauty and quality, but for its place in history. At the time of the name-change, the sons of Albion Morris who would build a company that has enhanced a recreational tradition were yet to be born.

"What if…"
(based on the cover image of the 1919 Morris catalog)

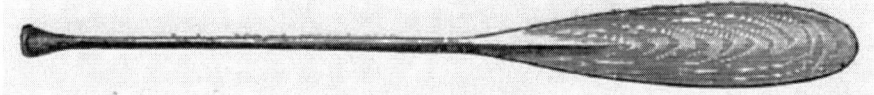

Paddle Strokes 1

Tracking the Journey…

I stumbled-upon the name-change from Fish to Morris while working on Bert and Charlie Morris's family tree. Believing there must have been a Morris someplace in the family, I reached far back into the Fish-line and found nobody named Morris. A discussion among those who share this family tree exists on *ancestry.com*, but none of the participants had a clue as to the reason for the change or the choice of the name "Morris". As one Morris-family descendant suggested, "maybe they just liked Morris better than Fish." Whatever the reason, it has been lost—and that may be the way those who changed their names would want it.

All historical information on the Fish-Morris family was carefully researched, much of it coming from original records found on *ancestry.com*.

Volume 20: p.37; NAME CHANGES OF MAINE RESIDENTS 1803-1892 compiled by Richard P. Roberts, transcribed verbatim from Acts and Resolves:

MARCH 22, 1856

Samuel Laine Fish   Samuel Morris   Veazie
Adalaide C. Fish, his wife   Adelaide Morris

Their minor children:
  John Fairfield Fish   John Morris
  Francis N. Fish   Francis Morris
  George W. Fish   George W. Morris
  Edward M. Fish   Edward Morris

MARCH 22, 1856 continued:

Silas Fish   Silas Morris   Leeds
Susan Fish, his wife   Susan Morris

Their minor children:
  Edwin W. Fish   Edwin W. Morris
  Alvin D. Fish   Alvin D. Morris

Seth Fish   Seth Morris
Abagail [sic] Fish, his wife   Abagail Morris

Their minor children:
  Seth Fish, junior   Seth Morris, junior
  Willard Fish   Willard Morris
  Mary Fish   Mary Morris

APRIL 1, 1856

Albion Mansfield Fish   Albion Morris   Veazie
Sophronia Kenada Fish,   Sophronia Morris
  his wife

Their children:
  Elizabeth Ellen Fish   Elizabeth Ellen Morris
  Isaac Livermore Fish   Isaac Livermore Morris
  Flora A. Fish   Flora A. Morris

The canoe image at the beginning of each chapter in this book is a logo used by Morris beginning in 1898. It appears on Morris receipts and stationary for more than a decade of the factory's existence. The tiny die that was used still exists in The Burr Company print shop in Bangor, as described by WCHA member Zip Kellogg in issue 166 of the journal *Wooden Canoe*. The image is a smaller version of that used in the 1901 Morris Catalog describing the Special Indian Extra Beam. This image was adopted by the Wooden Canoe Heritage Association in its emblem.

2

A HOME IN VEAZIE

The family was very skilled in the woodworking field. My dad could take a piece of wood and whittle just about anything you could imagine.
–Louis King, great-grandson of Charles Morris

Located in the lower central part of the state of Maine, the town of Veazie sits beside the Penobscot River, four miles north of Bangor. Originally considered part of Bangor, Veazie became a separate town in 1853 and was named for its most prominent and wealthy citizen. The town's main industry lay in lumber, using water-power from the Penobscot to operate sawmills. Samuel Laine Fish was a carpenter, so a lumber-producing town may have seemed a logical place to raise his growing family. Samuel was the youngest son born to a family of carpenters known to have built much of the town of Leeds, Maine; perhaps Sam felt it wise not to compete with his brothers for work. He moved his wife Adelaide and their four children to Veazie, building a house on Flagg Street in 1835. It was in this house that Samuel Fish established the business that supported a family which grew to nine children, and it was in this house that Samuel Fish Morris would die in 1873. It was here as well that his eldest son, Albion-- along with Sophronia Rollins Morris—would raise the youngest of their six children: canoe-builders Charles and Bert.

The house which sits today on Flagg Street in Veazie saw six generations of Fish-Morrises before passing from the bloodline of its original builder in 1974. Of a configuration typical in this part of New England, the house connects to a barn on its first and second floors via an ell; as such, it proved suitable for the Morris Canoe Company when it was in its infancy and, much later, the one-man-shop of semi-retired canoe-builder, Charles Morris. Initially, however, the house contained the carpentry shop of Charlie's grandfather, Samuel Laine Fish Morris, who passed the trade to his sons.

The main part of the house appears much as others in its day: a two-story, wood-frame structure with windows flanking each side of fancy double entry-doors, and three windows on the face of the upper story. The home's two chimneys once vented multiple woodstoves that heated the house before central heating was installed in the 1970s. The main rooms of the house each held a cast iron woodstove-- the most modern and efficient heating-method at the time. Today, attractive wood surrounds and mantles mark the place in each room where once a cast-iron stove stood—details which are among the legacies of Samuel Laine Morris.

From 1835, the house was a place of business as well as living. Like other homes of this era, there is no central hallway and one room leads to another. Evidence of its having housed several generations of carpenters begins on the second floor: after passing through several bedrooms on the way to the barn is a carpentry shop, its walls lined with shelves still holding remnants of the trade.

As tradesmen, the Morris family was part of America's growing middle class. The manner in which children were raised in the family of a tradesman differed from the ways of families where the father worked away from home. The boys born to Samuel Morris-- and later, to his son Albion-- were encouraged to work beside their father, helping him as they learned the tricks of his trade. The sons of Samuel Morris became woodworkers, carrying on a tradition that went back to the time when the family name was Fish.

The carpentry trade can be traced to Jirah Fish, a grandfather of Samuel Lane Fish Morris and the great-great grandfather of canoe-builders Bert and Charles Morris. Jirah was the second settler in what later became the town of Leeds, Maine. A carpenter, Jirah Fish built a frame house on the side of Fish Hill. His sons also became carpenters; the history of Leeds states that many of the early buildings of that town were built by members of the Fish family. Among them was the great-grandfather of Bert and Charles Morris, Seth Fish, who arrived April 12, 1803-- the second white child to be born in what is now Leeds. Seth would later take the name "Morris", as would his son Samuel. Of Samuel Morris's sons, Albion, John, Francis, and Edward are known to have taken up woodworking in one form or another, as did Albion's sons, Isaac Franklin, Charles, and Bert.

The Morris house sits on ground that stretches from Flagg Street to what was once called Orono Road, creating a large back-lot. Standing next to this was the home of the Freeman Rollins family, where on June 21, 1831, Sophronia Rollins was born. When she was seventeen, Sophronia married the dark-haired, blue-eyed neighbor-boy: twenty-two year old Albion Morris. The youngest of their six children would join the family tradition of woodworkers, specializing in canvas-covered canoes. At some time in the 1880s, the initial Morris factory was built on the lot behind the Morris barn, nestled between the houses where the parents of Bert and Charlie were raised.

Morris home on Flagg Street in Veazie in about 1930 (courtesy Ellen Waltz)

Map of Veazie, showing the relationship of the Morris home to that of the Rollins family

Paddle Strokes 2

Tracking the Journey...

Looking backward in their family tree, I found the ancestors of Charles and Bert Morris settled in New England during the seventeenth century and helped build the early communities of the European immigrants, participating in many of the historical events that shaped the American nation. This is one of the reasons behind the subtitle of this book, "Legacy of an American Family".

While most of the discussion herein concerns the male relatives of Bert and Charles Morris, women were there as well—quietly keeping things at home running smoothly. It was while traveling up Albion Morris's maternal line that I found a female ancestor who has been the subject of stories and paintings. Bert and Charlie's seventh-great-grandmother, Mary Chilton, is an American Legend: she is said to be the first woman to set foot on Plymouth Rock in 1620, at the age of thirteen.

Listed here is the Fish-Morris Ancestral Line of Bert and Charles Morris, with a bit about some of the men. Many of them were known to be carpenters, which is another of the reasons behind the subtitle of this book.

6X-great-Grandfather: Nathaniel Fish (1619-1693) born England died Sandwich MA—a founder of the town of Sandwich

5X-great-Grandfather: Ambrose Fish (1650-1691) born and died in Sandwich, MA

4X-great-Grandfather: Seth Fish (1682-1758) born and died in Sandwich, MA

3X-great-Grandfather: Benjamin Fish (1722-1759) born and died in Sandwich, MA

2X-great-Grandfather: Jirah Fish (1744-1821) born Sandwich, MA, died Leeds, ME; carpenter; Revolutionary War Veteran

Great-Grandfather: Seth (Fish) Morris (1782-1859) born Leeds, ME, died Leeds, ME; farmer and carpenter

Grandfather: Samuel Lane (Fish) Morris (1803-1873) born Leeds, ME, died Veazie, ME; carpenter; Captain in Aroostook War

Father: Albion (Fish) Morris (1826-1896) born Leeds, ME, died Veazie, ME; carpenter; Civil War Veteran

B.N. Morris (1865-1940) and Charles A. Morris (1860-1928)

Mary Chilton launches herself from a lapstrake boat onto Plymouth Rock
(illustration by F.T. Merrill now in the public domain)

Family-tree information was found using *ancestry.com*. Details regarding the men's lives were found in *History of the Town of Leeds, Androscoggin County, Maine, From Its Settlement June 10, 1780* by J. C. Stinchfield et al, and *History of Veazie* by Jean Hamilton, both of which are available on-line.

I'm grateful for the friendship of Bob Topliff, who permitted me to visit and explore the home he purchased from Charles King, the grandson of Charles Morris.

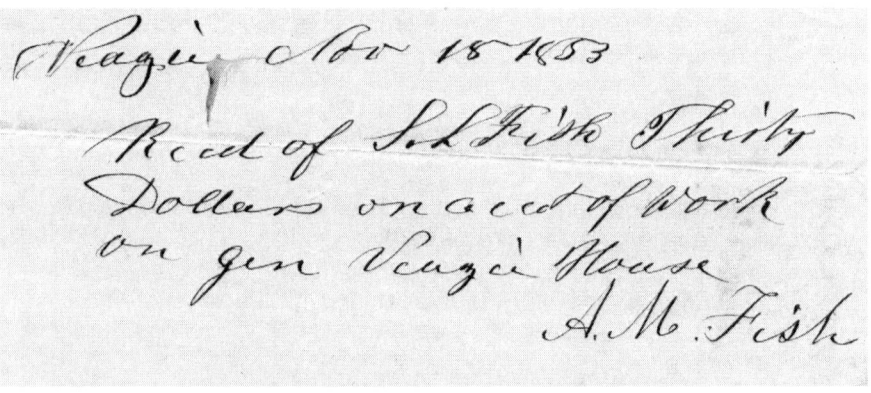

Receipt for payment by Samuel L. Fish (Morris) to Albion M. Fish (Morris) for work done on the home of General Veazie, November 18, 1853. We may assume this is Albion's handwriting.

Early photo of General Veazie's home,
from Jean Hamilton's *History of Veazie*

3

OFF TO WAR

The dead, the dead, the dead -- our dead -- or South or North, ours all -- our young men once so handsome and so joyous, taken from us -- the son from the mother, the husband from the wife, the dear friend from the dear friend...   --Walt Whitman, 1865

On July 12, 1861, at the age of thirty-five, Albion Morris entered the United States Army as a Musician with Company A, 2d Regiment Infantry, Maine Volunteers. It was not his first military experience: at the age of twelve, Albion Fish was part of Captain Samuel L. Fish's Company of infantry assigned to protect the Maine border in the Aroostook War, a dispute with no actual fighting. The American Civil War was quite a different thing.

Albion was the second of Samuel Morris's sons to volunteer for duty with the Union Army. Francis Napoleon Morris-- who went by the name "Frank"-- became a member of the 2d Regiment in Company F, when he volunteered at age twenty on May 28, 1861. Frank was first in the family to hold the rank of Musician-- essentially a non-combatant role, but one that saw the thick of battle.

The instrument Frank Morris played is unknown, but a sole musician assigned to a company might play either the bugle or snare drum. It is likely Frank played the drum like his brother Albion, a founding member of the Bangor Cornet Band. The Bangor Band was formed to provide entertainment for the citizenry and march in military and firemen's parades and musters. The entire city of Bangor turned out when Frank Morris and his fellow Maine 2d enlistees mustered in May of 1861. The Bangor Cornet Band led a parade of newly enlisted soldiers past cheering crowds through Bangor's streets. In less than two months, the Band would vote to enlist in the war as a group, becoming the Second Maine Regiment Band, and Albion Morris was among them.

Civil War snare drum (courtesy Bangor Historical Society)

Albion was already an accomplished drummer when he volunteered for the army. Approximately one soldier in forty-- on both the Northern and Southern sides of the conflict-- held the rank of Musician. Music was needed to inspire soldiers to battle, serving to unify them to one grand purpose; it filled empty-time with something that might lift the spirit of a man who longed to be elsewhere, helping to crowd the scenes of carnage from minds with memories of bloody conflict. It is known that on nights prior to engagement, bands on both sides played against each other, in a battle of the bands, and then led the march of troops onto the battlefield the following day.

As a Union drummer, Albion's drum was supported with a white strap. His blue army uniform frock coat fell nearly to his knees and was decorated with braid, known as a birdcage, in parallel lines across the front. A baldric, or decorative sling, crossed his chest from shoulder to waist. His Musician's sword hung from a leather frog on his belt; the sword designated for Musicians, a Model 1840, was similar to that carried by Noncommissioned Officers but with a shorter, twenty-six inch blade. On his head, Albion sported the traditional forage cap with bugle-symbol, designating him a member of the infantry.

A military snare-drummer was required to know thirty-eight different beats: fourteen for general use and twenty-four for marching cadence. A drummer marched to the right of a column of men. At a time prior to the walkie-talkie, the drummer served to convey marching-orders, and as such, was a prime target. However, Albion Morris was a member of the full twenty-four-member military band which accompanied his regiment rather than the two-man band assigned to the company, which consisted of a drummer and either a bugler or fifer.

As the war dragged on and men were needed to fight, the Civil War military bands did not remain intact. Although it appears Albion Morris drummed throughout his military service, Musicians could be ordered to pick up a gun and join the battle or to leave the battlefield and assist surgeons. During his two years with the Second Maine, Albion's brother, Frank, was involved in several of the war's bloodiest battles, including First and Second Bull Run (Manassas), Antietam and Fredericksburg. Albion Morris and nine other members of the Bangor

Band followed the Second Maine Infantry through the campaigns of General McClellan and the Peninsula Campaign.

In his book *To The Gates of Richmond*, Stephan Sears shares the following description of the battle that took place May 5, 1862 at Fair Oaks during the battle at Williamsburg, which was part of the Peninsula Campaign:

[Federal] Corps commander [Samuel] Heintzelman joined the desperate struggle to close the broken ranks. He hit on the novel idea of rallying them with music. Finding several regimental bands standing by bewildered as the battle closed in, Heintzelman ordered them to take up their instruments. "Play! Play! It's all you're good for," he shouted. "Play, damn it! Play some marching tune! Play 'Yankee Doodle,' or any doodle you can think of, only play something!" Before long, over the roar of the guns, came the incongruous sound of "Yankee Doodle" and then "Three Cheers for the Red, White, and Blue." One of [General Joseph] Hooker's men thought the music was worth a thousand men. "It saved the battle," he wrote.

Although Albion and Frank held the rank of Musician, as the war raged-on it is reasonable to assume the brothers may have been put to use retrieving wounded from the battlefield and assisting as needed within the hospital tents. Frank Morris was with the Bangor Infantry when they fought the Battle of Fredericksburg on December 11-15 1862, where Union losses were twice that of Confederate.

It was at Fredericksburg that the future author of *Little Women*, Louisa May Alcott, worked as a nurse; she would later use this experience as the basis of her book, *Hospital Sketches*. Poet Walt Whitman also tended the sick and injured at Fredericksburg, an experience he would share through powerful words that influenced the way poetry has since been written. It is possible Frank Morris crossed paths with Alcott and Whitman. The Morris brothers likely shared duties similar to theirs during the war, the memories of which undoubtedly remained with them throughout their lives.

> *...Thus in silence in dreams' projections,*
> *Returning, resuming, I thread my way through the hospitals,*
> *The hurt and wounded I pacify with soothing hand,*
> *I sit by the restless all the dark night, some are so young,*
>   *Some suffer so much, I recall the experience sweet and sad...*
>   --Walt Whitman

Albion Morris originally enlisted for a term of three years but was honorably discharged August 11, 1862 after serving only one, as an Act of Congress abolished the bands assigned to volunteer regiments. Records show Albion mustered-out of the Second Regiment with twenty-four fellow musicians. Nearly a month later, on September 10th, Eighteen-year-old George Washington Morris followed his older brothers into battle, but not as a non-combatant. He was assigned to Company B of Maine's twenty-second infantry, organized in Bangor, Maine, mustering October 10, 1862 for nine months' service under the command of Colonel Simon G. Jerrard. His unit was sent to Louisiana, where they were involved in the Siege of Port Hudson from June 1 to July 8, 1863.

When Frank Morris and the rest of the Maine Second mustered out June 4, 1863, crowds in Bangor greeted their return and a ceremony was held at Norumbega Hall. But the youngest member of the Morris family to enter the fight was not so fortunate; on July 3, 1863, George

Washington Morris died of wounds at the Siege of Port Hudson. He was nineteen years old and one of only eight enlisted men in the Maine Twenty-second listed as killed or mortally wounded at a place where most death happened due to disease.

"The Battle of Port Hudson" by J.O. Davidson (image in the public domain)

At the time of George Morris's death, the federal government assumed no responsibility toward those who died in service; no provision existed for gathering the dead and transporting them home. Families heard of bodies buried in haste, in shallow, unmarked graves-- if buried at all. Records show George was buried the day he died.

Traditionally, care of the dead was a family-responsibility: people died in familiar surroundings, in the presence of those they loved-- often in the arms of one who held them dear. Mothers bathed the bodies of children they had borne, dressed them in their Sunday-best, and laid them in the parlor so all could bid them good-bye. But in this time of Civil War, men died in great numbers, far from home; information on the dead was slow to reach families and could be incorrect. It is unknown when the family of George Morris learned of his death. We can assume the Morris family not only felt grief at his loss but also discomfort from lack of closure. George's name was added to a memorial headstone in the Morris burial plot in Veazie, where those who loved George Washington Morris could be certain that the memory of this blond-haired, blue-eyed boy was preserved close to home. Following the war, Frank Morris would move West, settling first in Nevada and later in California; he would marry and support a growing family as a carpenter. His eldest son would be named George Washington Morris.

On July 7, 1864, Albion Morris volunteered for a two-month stretch as a Musician in the Maine State Guards; then on March 15, 1865, as the war was winding down, Albion enlisted a third time: with the 14th Volunteer Infantry Regiment, bound for provost duty in Savannah, Georgia. Again he enlisted with members of the Bangor Cornet Band. Albion and nine other members of the band had served the Second Maine, under the direction of Americus D. Harlow. Harlow was commissioned as an officer and achieved the rank of First Lieutenant in Company I, Maine 14th Infantry Regiment, mustering with Albion Morris and other band members on March 22, 1865, and again forming a regimental band.

Perhaps re-enlistment at this time was more to Albion Morris than an obligation to Maine and to fellow band members; perhaps it seemed a means of learning more about his brother George's death. The

14th Maine had also fought at Port Hudson and Albion may have hoped to locate men who would share stories of the battle, shedding light on the last days of George Morris. He may have hoped to locate the grave and pay homage to this brother who would not be returning home, reassuring members of the Morris family that George Washington Morris rested safely, among other brave men.

It is unknown whether Albion spoke to anyone who knew anything of the Siege of Port Hudson or of George's death, and it's unlikely he was anywhere near the place where his brother was buried. The 14th Maine marched to Augusta, Georgia, from May 6th to 14th, then returned to Savannah between May 31st and June 7th, moving on to Darien over the ninth and tenth. All three cities lie on the Eastern side of Georgia, approximately seven hundred miles from Baton Rouge, where George had died. The regiment mustered out in Bangor on August 28, 1865. It was during this third tour of duty that Albion Morris contracted malaria, from which he would suffer chronically, drawing a government pension as an invalid from February 12, 1887 until his death October 2, 1896.

In 1867, the place where the Union dead were buried following the Siege of Port Hudson became the National Cemetery at Baton Rouge. It is here that George W. Morris rests, beneath a white stone that stands among rows of identical markers and is decorated with a small American flag each Memorial Day.

Grave of George Washington Morris (1844-1863) in Baton Rouge National Cemetery (image submitted to Find-A-Grave by Diane Owens and used with her permission)

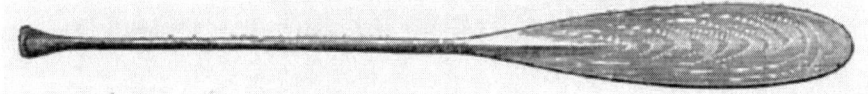

Paddle Strokes 3

Tracking the Journey...

The military records of Albion, Francis, and George Morris found in the Maine State Archives in Augusta contain more detail than records found on line through ancestry.com, including physical descriptions. Additional details of Albion Morris's Civil War enlistment involve a serendipitous discovery. I was browsing a card catalog in the Bangor Library with Greg Nolan at my side, when his eyes fell on a book in a nearby shelf: *Music and Musicians of Maine.* I had already discovered that Albion Morris served as a musician during the war and that, at the time of his death, he was considered to have been the best snare drummer in the state. His enlistment with the other band members, described in the book Greg spied, shed light not only on Albion as a man but on the times and the place in which he lived.

Although Albion and his family lived in Bangor, records included in *History of the Town of Leeds* indicate Sophronia and the children may have received financial assistance from Albion's birthplace of Leeds while he was away at war. On July 6, 1861, a special meeting was held in Leeds to make "ample provision for the families of their Soldier Boys in Blue." The selectmen were "authorized to draw... such sums of money as might be necessary for the support and comfort of the families of those who had gone into or should subsequently go into the United States service." It is unknown what "support and comfort" Sophronia and the children received. Support at the time of Albion's initial enlistment came partly from donations made by those who were unable to volunteer. Later, bounties of from $75 to $400 were offered in order that the town reach its quota of men, and bonds were sold to help the town pay this debt.

In 1877 "Cornet" was dropped from the Bangor Cornet Band's name, making it The Bangor Band-- which is still in existence as one of the oldest community bands in the United States.

Port Hudson is the site of the longest siege in American history during the American Civil War and was designated a National Historic Landmark on May 30, 1974. Living history re-enactments are held there each year.

Documentation of Albion Morris's initial enlistment in the Union Army, with interesting descriptive information. The other two enlistments have him slightly taller, at 5'7". Albion was 35 years old at this enlistment, not 33 as stated.

Soldier's Dream by Currier and Ives

Military record of George Washington Morris

Documentation of young George's burial (found on-line through ancestry.com)

Draft registration for Frank Morris; note he is listed as a Joiner, indicating that at age 20 he had a high degree of skill as a carpenter. (found on line through ancestry.com)

Name.	Morris, Frank N.	Age.	Co.	Inf.	Cav.	Heavy Art'y.
		20	F	2nd		

Rank.	Private – Musician –		Married Single.	Complexion.	Eyes.

Enlisted.	May 28, 1861	Mustered. May 28, 1861	Years 2	Mo's	Occupation.	Hair.

Born.		Residence. Leeds.	Ft.	In.	Pages. 1193 –
					1232 – 1311 –

Left Service. June 4, 1863	How Left Service. M.O. & hon. disch'd.	1336 – 1273
Muster-Out-To-Date. 186_	Reenlisted.	1274 – 1288 –

Transferred To	Previous Service.

Where Mustered In. Willett's Point, N.Y.	Where Mustered Out. Bangor.

Remarks.

Military record of Francis Napoleon Morris; he was living in the Flagg Street home with his parents when he enlisted and saw the thick of battle in the war. Frank lived to be 73. He is buried in San Francisco where he rests under a Civil War headstone.

Resources:

Edwards, George Thornton, *Music and Musicians of Maine*, The Southworth Press, Portland, Maine, 1928, pp.337-339.

Sears, Stephen, *The Gates of Richmond*, First Mariner Books, 1991.

Mundy, James H., *Second to None, The Story of the 2nd Maine Volunteer Infantry: "The Bangor Regiment"*, Scarborough, Maine: Harp Publications, 1992.

History of the Town of Leeds, Androscoggin County, Maine, From Its Settlement June 10, 1780, by J. C. Stinchfield et al, is available on line at https://archive.org/details/historyoftownofl00stinrich

Military records were found in the Maine State Archives in Augusta, where staff was very helpful.

4

THE CANOE BUILDERS ARRIVE

The way of a canoe is the way of the wilderness, and of a freedom almost forgotten.   —Sigurd Olson

Charles A. Morris was born February 10, 1860, the fourth child and third son of Albion and Sophronia Morris. His eldest sister, Elizabeth Ellen, born in 1848, was followed by Isaac Franklin in 1852, Flora in 1853 and Albion Junior in 1858. As they were close in age, we may assume Charlie and his brother Albie played together. Albion Jr. might have become another canoe-building-Morris-brother had be not died; the little boy appears as a two-year-old in the 1860 census but isn't there in 1870, indicating he died sometime in the 1860s-- possibly due to one of the many things that took the lives of children prior to the discovery of antibiotics. His death undoubtedly compounded the concerns of the Morris family during a decade of political unrest, family separations and loss.

Bert Morris was born ten months after his father's return from the war, on June 24, 1866; he was eighteen years younger than his eldest sister and six years younger than Charlie. Little Bert's arrival might have seemed a blessing to parents who had been separated by war and lost a child: proof that all was again right, now that Papa was returned to his family. Their new little son came into the world at a time of peace, at the tail-end of a number of children. The little boy may have been doted-upon by sisters who would rather play with a real baby than a doll. He was known affectionately as "Bertie" then, and the name stuck with him into generations of family who never met him in-person. It seems Bert Morris was appreciated from the beginning and remembered fondly after he was gone.

Albion Morris continued to work as a finish carpenter and cabinet maker until late in his life, when the effects of malaria contracted during the war confined him to bed. A record of his work, written in elegant handwriting, indicates he was making three dollars a day in 1868-- about twice the going wage. Additionally, Albion is known to have built showcases for use in shops. Albion Morris's children were at hand, and, as with other tradesmen and the farmers of his day, his sons learned from him and shared in the work from their early years. In the nineteenth century, this was not the custom for all fathers.

It was a tradition for boys at this time in history to be dressed in the manner of their sisters and remain in the domain of their mothers— having little contact with their fathers-- until beginning a process known as "breeching" at approximately the age of six. While the young son of a doctor or college professor might not have much contact with his father, this was not the case with tradesmen who accomplished some of the work of their trade in the family home. Bert Morris probably learned the names of his papa's tools and assisted with projects while still in skirts. It was customary for a man with a trade to take his son under his wing and determine the boy's interest in the craft. By the time Little Bertie was old enough to wield a hammer, Charlie Morris would have been their father's helpful assistant and big brother Isaac Franklin Morris was getting jobs on his own.

It is possible that young Bertie idolized his big brother Charlie, following him into the carpentry shop of their father, watching closely and listening carefully as the older boy learned the work. It's likely that Albion Morris believed the future of each of his sons was assured, as his skill as a finish carpenter and cabinet maker was passed to all his sons-- and Bertie Morris not only learned from him, but was mentored by his brothers as well. The sons of Albion Morris attended school through the eighth grade and then took up the family trade in earnest.

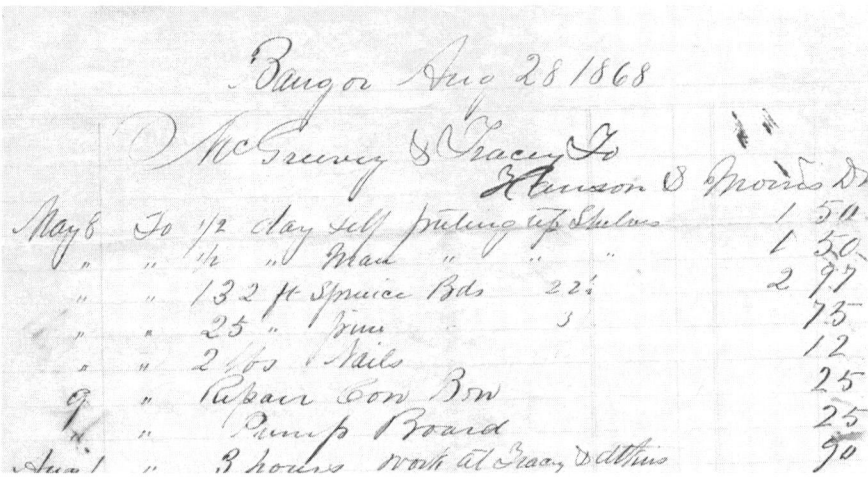

Detail of bill for services rendered by Albion Morris, found in the Flagg Street house

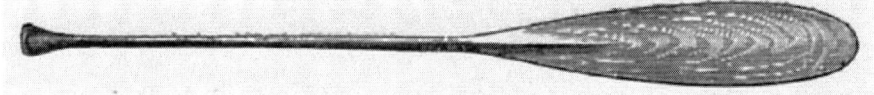

Paddle Strokes 4

Tracking the Journey...

A human life is bracketed by a pair of events: one's birth and one's death. The dates of those events belong to a person as much as their name, as much as the experiences that happen in between. --Kate Morton

Albion Morris Junior is someone I'd like to know better. The only written record of his existance I've found as of this writing is his name in the 1860 census, where he appears twice. The family moved and were enumerated on two separate occasions (so much for the U.S. Census being a truly accurate accounting). He isn't buried in the Veazie cemetery with his grandparents or in Bangor's Mount Hope, where his parents rest beside his brothers Charlie and Bert, and brother Isaac Franklin is across the way. Albion and Sophronia Morris and their children were living in Bangor in 1860, and Little Albie may be in one of three small, old cemeteries listed on-line without any details. Knowing the family lost this little son adds much to their story, and knowing when and how his death occurred may say more. I intend to follow up on this in another trip to Maine.

5

BEGINNINGS

There is nothing, absolutely nothing
Half so much worth doing
As simply messing about in boats.

--Ratty, *The Wind in the Willows*

Writers of fact, fiction, or philosophy are more easily understood long after they have departed this earth, as the words left behind permit a grasp on the individual. Often such a person has written in journals, and correspondence with others remains intact. If a person achieved importance in their own time, contemporaries may have composed biographies or submitted articles about them to the media. And so, we come to understand such people and their contribution to the times in which they lived through a written legacy.

Charles and Bert Morris were not writers. They may have been philosophers, but their philosophy was set into wood, covered in canvas, and launched upon water. They were businessmen: entrepreneurs in an age of invention and discovery and increased leisure time. The story of the Morris brothers is found not only in wood and canvas canoes which continue to be enjoyed nearly a century after the factory ceased production, but also in the many ways these canoes and the business practices surrounding them contributed to a future in which the paddling sports are an important aspect of recreation.

The eldest Morris brother, Isaac Franklin Morris (who went by

"Frank"), is listed in the 1870 census as a carpenter. He may have assisted in some manner with the canoe business developed by his younger siblings, but no documentation of this has been discovered. Frank was eight years older than Charles and fourteen years older than Bert, and his career was well underway before his younger brothers might have begun experimenting with canoe-building. Frank Morris spent his life in the Bangor area, where he married in 1875 and raised his children. City directory information states he was an employee of Morse and Company of Bangor, manufacturers of lumber and building trim. Perhaps Frank directed some first-grade lumber into the hands of his boat-building-brothers and occasionally lent a helping hand at the factory.

In the mid-1880s, Charlie Morris married Grace Grimby, and in 1888 their daughter, Gladys, was born. The family made the Flagg Street house their home; it was customary for at least one child to assist aging parents, and the effects of his wartime malarial infection had gradually rendered Albion Morris an invalid. *The Maine Register* for this time lists Charles Morris as a carriage maker, and he is also known to have built coffins--but it seems he was also tinkering with boats. Charlie had a cottage on near-by Pushaw Lake, where he kept a lapstrake fishing boat he'd built for himself.

The precise time and manner in which the Morris brothers became canoe builders isn't known. While it can be shown that 1892 is a reliable date for the establishment of the business at the State Street location, Bert-- and his brother Charlie—were building and selling boats before B.N. Morris Canoes was an advertised commercial venture.

At some point in the 1880s, a fifty-by-eighty-foot building was erected behind the family's barn on Flagg Street. This first official Morris Factory is described in Jean Hamilton's *History of Veazie* as being four stories high, with each floor devoted to a separate stage in canoe-building. According to Charlie's great-grandson Louie King, this building remained the place where ribs were milled even after construction of the factory complex on State Street. The lot containing the Flagg Street house reaches all the way to the street behind it, and it is likely this first factory building faced that street for ease of entry and exit. Aside from the space where it once stood, no trace of this building exists today.

Sign that once graced the Morris canoe shop behind the Flagg Street home.
(courtesy Dave Topliff)

Rushton was building beautiful all-wood boats, and the rowboat Charles Morris created for his own use was of lapstrake design. Down the Penobscot River in Bangor, Evan Gerrish had been selling canvas-covered canoes at least since the early as the 1880s, and E.M. White in nearby Old Town followed close-behind. Perhaps the thought of building boats commercially began with someone admiring the rowboat Charlie built for himself, and a request that he build one for some extra money. In his carriage and coffin-making trade, Charles Morris learned the advantages of producing a product that might draw people to his door, rather than having to go door-knocking to drum up business as a carpenter. This advantage was not lost on Bert Morris.

The July 6, 1889 edition of the *Bangor Daily Whig and Courier* contains a list of exhibitors at a July 4th celebration. It states, "B. N. Morris, Veazie, 1 wagon containing canoes of his make." This is the earliest-known mention in contemporary print of Bert Morris as a canoe builder. A wagonload of canoes indicates he was producing at more than the hobby-level. He would have been twenty-three years old. By 1890, advertisements for B.N. Morris canoes began to appear in national publications: the May 1, 1890 *Forest and Stream* contains the earliest national advertisement for Morris canoes known to me, displaying a simple canoe profile with "B. N. Morris, Manufacturer of Canvas Canoes. Factory in Veazie, Me."

1891 saw the first evidence of a contract between Morris and an agent offering to sell their canoes: L.W. Ferdinand, Boston wholesaler and retailer of ship's chandlery and hardware, listed B.N. Morris canoes in an advertisement in *Forest and Stream* and included Morris canoes in their catalog.

CANVAS COVERED CANOES.

No.	Length	beam		each
1,	15 ft.	29 inches amidship,	with two paddles,	$32.00
2,	15½	30	"	33.00
3,	16	30	"	34.00
4,	16½	31	"	35.00
5,	17	31	"	37.00
6,	18	32	"	39.50
7,	18½	33	"	41.00
8,	19½	34	"	42.00

Indian model Morris canoe, as offered in the 1891 L.W. Ferdinand catalog; note the odd half-sizes

B. N. Morris, Manufacturer of Canvas Canoes.
Factory at Veazie, Me.

L. W. FERDINAND & CO., Agents, Boston.

1891 ad in *Forest and Stream*; L.W. Fredinand was the first of Morris's many agents

Initially, the factory building behind the Morris barn may have been part of Charlie's carriage-building operation. By 1892, property with plenty of room for expansion of a growing business had been purchased, and buildings were going up: the Sixth Annual Report of the *Maine Bureau of Industrial and Labor Statistics Manual*, 1892, shows construction of a new boat and canoe factory in Veazie for $3000. It was on State Street, around the corner from the Morris family home, beside the railroad tracks, near the majestic Penobscot River.

Early image of Morris factory complex; center building with mansard roof was the office.

In naming the canoe business, the reason for choosing Bert's name over Charlie's is unknown; it may be that Charlie initially had little to do with the canoe-building business other than providing inspiration, advice and an occasional helping hand. It seems Charles Morris preferred to continue producing carriages and coffins and let Bert follow his passion for boat building as a profession. The young, unmarried Bert might have been more inclined to take financial risks than his older brother, who continued to be listed in city directories as a carriage builder into the 1890s.

The large B.N. Morris factory complex, where approximately twenty thousand boats would be constructed during the first two decades of the twentieth century, began with a single building that held the office of the B.N. Morris Company on the first floor and an apartment on the second. With its mansard roofline, this building appears older than the gable-roofed factory buildings that would succumb to fire by 1920; it probably already existed on the land at the time of purchase, and Bert Morris moved in. In the nineteen-teens this building would more than double in size, stretching from a square box, one window-deep on each side, to a rectangular structure five windows-deep. It would survive the factory fire and remain Bert's home until his death in 1940. The building stands today, as the office of The Stucco Lodge Motel.

The canoe factory complex constructed on State Street in Veazie which initially cost $3,000 ($80K in 2014 dollars) and employed six men would be expanded over the 28 years of its existence. Ten years later, in 1902, another $1500 ($42K in 2014 dollars) was put into the factory, which then employed 25 men. As the factory grew, so did its address: 50 State Street became 112 State Street, then 145, then 205, and finally 240. The address of the building that survived the fire is currently 1382 State Street.

In 1892, advertisements for B.N. Morris canoes in *Forest and Stream* suggest canoeing "for pleasure" and mention a catalog. The earliest known existing Morris catalog, dated 1893, offers fifteen canvas-covered boats and canoes—many with fancy decks comprised of alternating strips of wood and other elements similar to those found on the all-wood vessels of J.H. Rushton.

An 1893 advertising flyer included with the catalog describes six Morris canoes that were displayed at the World's Columbian Exposition in Chicago: a Canadian paddling canoe, a sailing canoe, a paddling cruiser, a Penobscot River skiff, a yacht tender, and the Indian model paddling canoe. The 15 foot Sailing Canoe is described as having mahogany decks and a 7 foot cockpit. The 14 foot Paddling Cruiser also has a 7 foot cockpit. The 18 foot canvas-covered "Penobscot River Skiff" has 8 foot decks of alternating strips of oak and cherry, four "cane-woven thwarts" (perhaps an early version of the Morris cane-filled seat) and two rowing stations. The 11 foot Yacht Tender also has long decks set with strips of oak and cherry and sitting thwarts filled with cane. The Indian Model Paddling Canoe is 16 feet long and 36 inches wide, with 24 inch decks at each end and "cane woven thwarts". It is described as having "oak stems and keel built in similar manner" to the other boats in the collection.

```
643. Morse & Co., Bath, Me. Model of        664. Rogers, William, Bath, Me. Model
     steamer "B. W. Morse" and barge "Inde-       of ship "Gov. Robie."    E gal. 35    528
     pendent."              E gal. 35   528  665. Rooke, George, Emporia, Kansas.
644. Meaney, John, Boston. Race boat             Working steam models of boats without
     equipment.             E gal. 46   532       bows.                   E gal. 46    529
645. Morris, B. N., Veazie, Maine.           666. Rushton, J. H., Canton, N. Y.
      a Boats and canoes.   E gal. 45   528       E gal. 31-32
      b Boat equipment.                 532        a Row and sail boats; canoes.       528
646. Neumann, Rudolph, Unalaska, Alas-             b Fittings for small boats.         532
     ka. Hatch bidarka (skin canoe) complete      For exhibit see page 878.
     —Aleutian Islands. Bydarka and outfit of 667. Safety Car Heating & Lighting Co.,
     hunting sled, paddles. etc. — Morton        New York. Gas buoys.     J-3         534
     Sound. Birch bark canoe (outfit com-    668. Sewall, A.. & Co., Bath, Me. Model
     plete), double birch bark canoe (outfit     of ship "Rappahannock."  E gal. 36   528
```

Detail of Columbian Exposition directory, showing B.N. Morris opposite J.H. Rushton; E.H. Gerrish is on the proceeding page

The World's Columbian Exposition, also known as the Chicago World's

Fair, celebrated the 400th anniversary of the arrival of Christopher Columbus in the New World in 1492. This was the first time Morris exhibited a boat based on the native canoe in an international arena—an unintended nod in the direction of Native American People in a place celebrating the arrival of the Europeans.

Entrance to the Transportation Building, World's Columbian Exposition

Situated in the Transportation Building near fellow canoe builders Evan Gerrish and J.H. Rushton, the Morris men not only had an opportunity to compare offerings but to peruse exhibits such as Machines for Working Wood, which included molding and carving machines, electric lathes, grinders and pattern makers' machines. Brochures for the fair incorporate images of huge factories with multiple chimneys belching smoke. By 1900, Charles Morris would be listed in the U.S. census as a machinist at the B.N. Morris plant and images of that plant would show chimneys streaming smoke. During the decade of the 1890s, the Morris Company would move from a time when a canoe was made by one man using hand-tools, toward use of a mechanized system involving many men, each assigned to a portion of the canoe-building process.

Many hands and machines making work light at the Morris factory c.1910. Bert is the fellow on the left, in the suit and hat, in this photo of the Woodworking Machine Room.

Factory hands working the machinery in the Morris Rib Mill. Bert stands in the rear on the right (above images from an undated Morris catalog reprinted by the Wooden Canoe Heritage Association in 1982)

The Indian model canoe would become Morris's standard-- the basis for the majority of boats built by B.N. Morris until the factory fire in 1919. It is doubtful that many of the other boats offered by Morris in their 1893 catalog were ever made. A stock market crash that spring plunged the economy into a depression that would last until 1897; with the country in an economic depression, the simple canvas-covered Indian model canoe was what sold. B.N. Morris became a company that primarily produced canvas-covered canoes of one distinct type.

In contrast, the fair in Chicago nearly ruined J.H. Rushton, whose all-wood boats were expensive and not as easily maintained as a simple canvas-covered canoe built of component parts. In *Rushton and His Times in American Canoeing,* Atwood Manley states that the Columbian Exposition and the depression that began in 1893 reduced Rushton to near-poverty for a period of five years.

Morris factory workers c.1900; Charlie is believed to be the fellow on the left (with paddle), and Bert on the right, with Ella Morris standing behind him (courtesy Daniel Miller)

In addition to having responsibility for his parents in their old age, Charles Morris became a widower on October 31, 1893, when his wife Gracie died of a ruptured appendix at the family cabin on Pushaw Lake. The final day of the World's Fair in Chicago was October 30th, and whether Charlie was at the cabin with Gracie or in-transit from Chicago is unknown. Grace Grimby Morris had celebrated her 28th birthday less than two weeks earlier. Bert's relatively new business-interest was unfolding at a time of economic instability, and with his family responsibilities, Charles Morris may have felt relief knowing his name wasn't attached to the enterprise.

Detail of Bert and Ella from Morris factory workers (p. 47)

Bert Morris would remain a single man until October 15, 1898, when, at the age of 32, he married 22-year-old Ella Page of Veazie. Ella is likely the young woman standing behind Bert in a turn of the century photograph of Morris factory workers (pp. 47-48). Little can be found regarding Ella Page Morris. Her obituary in the *Bangor Daily Commercial* states she died January 30, 1917, in Boston of an ailment that "came on suddenly". By that time, she and Bert had been divorced for several years. Ella is buried in the Page family plot in Veazie.

Bert and stenographer Margaret Pierce were married by a Justice of the Peace in Portsmouth, New Hampshire, on October 23, 1917; he was 51 and she, 31. Bert's marriages to younger women suggests he was hoping for an heir, which may not have been possible due to his exposure to white lead. The dangers of heavy metal exposure were barely being explored in the nineteenth century; it is now known that lead poisoning can affect fertility. The process of building canvas covered boats involves the use of a formulation on the canvas to fill the weave of the cloth and make it waterproof. Filler-formulas vary, but generally consist of linseed oil, mineral spirits, paint, silica and, at that time, included white lead as a mildewcide.

The fact that Bert Morris fathered no children suggests he had his hands in white lead as a young man-- perhaps in his teens-- while he worked to produce and perfect the canoe bearing his name; once the factory on State Street was in full-swing, he was in charge of its management, putting his time into promoting the product that others built under his direction.

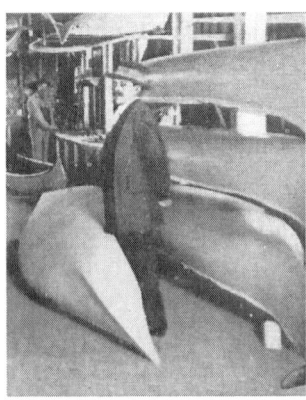

Bert supervises in his factory's filling room, where factory hands have their hands in the filler (image from undated Morris catalog reprinted by the WCHA in 1982)

Bert Morris takes advantage of a photo-op at the factory (image from undated Morris catalog reprinted by the WCHA in 1982)

Detail of above

The Morris Canoe

Workers in one of the factory's finishing rooms (image from undated Morris catalog reprinted by the WCHA in 1982)

Morris factory complex c.1900 (center) and in 1917, showing chimneys belching smoke (courtesy *The Historic Wood Canoe and Boat Manufacturer Catalog Collection* edited by Daniel Miller and Benson Gray)

Paddle Strokes 5

Tracking the Journey...

A variety of "start-dates" for the Morris Company exist within the company's self-promotional literature and in sources based upon this literature, where the information cannot be verified or which contradicts other, more reliable, information.

Among the information that seems "entirely wrong" is a statement in a 1953 pamphlet published by the Veazie Congregational Church, saying that in 1882 Charles Morris started a business he named The Veazie Canoe Company. The 1882 *Maine Register* shows Albion Morris as a carpenter and Charles as a carriage maker. In the 1880 census Bert is described as being "at school" and Charlie is engaged in "day labor". There was a Veazie Canoe Company, which appeared in about 1905 as a way of marketing a less expensive Morris Canoe. A thorough search of the files of Bangor's newspapers and other periodicals from the pre-1900 time-period has turned up no mention of a Veazie Canoe Company; as of this writing, there is nothing beyond statements written long after the fact-- such as that found in the Veazie church's booklet-- to support the existence of an earlier Veazie Canoe Company. Naming a canoe company after a place rather than a person would have been unusual in the 1880s.

In some of his 20th Century catalogs, Bert Morris states that he first advertised in *Field and Stream* magazine in 1887. *Field and Stream* didn't exist until 1895. Thinking he might have meant *Forest and Stream*, I went through every issue of the magazine for 1887 and found no ad for Morris Canoes. The earliest ad found so-far for Morris canoes is in the May 1, 1890 *Forest and Stream* (thanks must go to Howard Herman-Haase for finding this).

The 1916 Morris catalog states that "the Morris canvas-covered canoes have been on the market for 26 years", putting the start date at 1890. However, advertisements in the March 1916 *Hunter-Trader-Trapper* and the May 1916 *McClure's* contain the phrase "established 1891".

WCHA webmaster and *Wooden Canoe* editor, Dan Miller, found mention of Morris in *The Rudder*, Vol. 1, No. 8, January 1891, in a statement that reads: "B.N. Morris, of Veazie, Maine, is anxious to build a war-canoe. He says a canvas war-canoe will beat a wood-built Ho-ho-ho-ko hands down." Bert had great faith in his canvas boats.

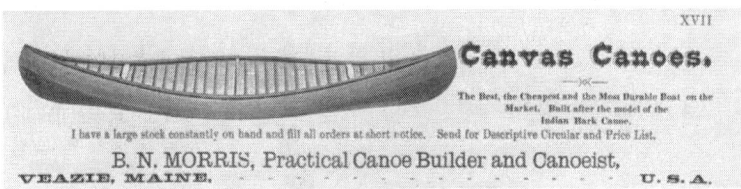

Advertisement in *Rudder*, 1892

The *Maine Register* contains no mention of B.N. Morris in 1891, but in 1892 identifies him as a manufacturer of canvas canoes in Veazie. Bert's 1940 obituary in the *Bangor Daily News* gives an 1892 start-date.

An August 17, 1912 *Bangor Daily Commercial* article regarding Morris boats, includes the statement that "the Morris canvas-covered canoes have been on the market 21 years..." indicating a start-date of 1891.

Photo taken behind the barn on Flagg Street—I am standing where the first Morris factory once existed, looking at the back of the barn and admiring beautiful cedar shingle-work installed by Morris men. From this perspective, it is difficult to imagine the original factory building stood four stories high as reported in Ms. Hamilton's book, *The History of Veazie*, as such a structure would have towered over everything in the neighborhood; three stories would have been a tall building in this location. My guess is that the building was three stories, was remembered as being "very tall", and such memories stretched the building to four stories. None of the buildings comprising the Morris plant on State Street were more than three stories high.

6

THE INDIAN MODEL AND ITS DESCENDANTS

Unequalled for beauty of line an general all around utility, the Eastern woodlands canoe, and in particular the canoe of the eastern central or Abenaki group (Tetes de Boule, St. Frances-Kennebec-Maliseet) became the form of the modern factory-built canvas canoes... Though Adney mourned the passing of a great canoe-building tradition, he believed that this tradition was finding new life in the "carpentered" factory canoes of the Peterborough region of Ontario and the cedar/canvas canoes of Maine... –John Jennings, Bark Canoes: the Art and Obsession of Tappan Adney

Ferdy Goode's Abenaki-style birch bark rests in front of a c.1910 Morris.

Aside from information in eleven existing Morris catalogs, there are no written records documenting changes in design of the Morris canoe. This leaves the canoes themselves to tell the story, which was the logic behind the development of a database containing information on as many Morris canoes as possible. Denis Kallery and I began collecting data in 2007, asking WCHA members to forward information on their own canoes and any they spotted in-person or on line. As of 2015, the database consists of more than three hundred Morris canoes, and they have had much to share.

While it seems the Morris changed little in the thirty years between 1890 and 1920, database canoes show minor changes that help us understand the evolution of the Morris.

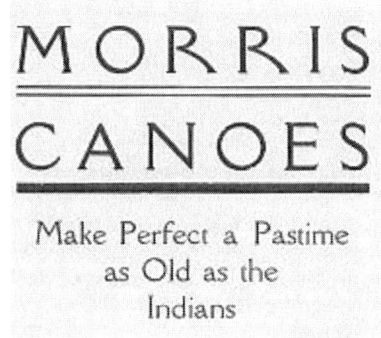

From a Morris brochure c.1910

The Morris Catalogs

Eleven Morris catalogs are known to exist and are included in *The Historic Wood Boat and Canoe Manufacturer Catalog Collection* edited by Daniel Miller and Benson Gray, a collection of over 200 catalogs from more than fifty manufacturers, available on flash drive from the WCHA Store. I have consolidated information on the models using descriptive information from the catalogs, adding what the canoes themselves appear to indicate.

Four Morris catalogs are undated, but have been carefully scrutinized by Dan Miller and Benson Gray and are listed with the years they were most-likely produced. The B.N. Morris catalogs that are known to exist are as follows:

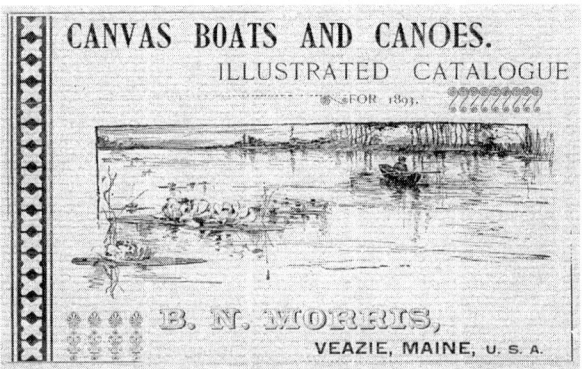

1893 Catalog published by J.H. Bacon of Bangor consisting of 28 pages, the last three of which contain advertising for Calman's Elastic Spar Varnish, *Gameland* magazine, *The Rudder, Sail and Paddle* magazine, a fish lure called KATCH=EM, L.W. Fredinand & Co. (dealers in chandlery), Yawman & Erbe's Automatic Reel, and Pflueger's Luminous Fish Baits. Presumably the ads helped cover the cost of publishing. Cover is yellow.

1901-1902 Catalog consisting of 16 pages; cover is gray.

1903 Catalog consisting of 16 pages, the last two of which advertise Morris agents H.& D. Folsum Arms and the J. Stevens Arms and Tool Company. Cover is red.

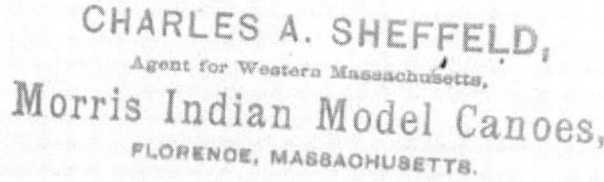

Morris agent's stamp is an interesting addition to this catalog

1911 Catalog with original mailing envelope, consisting of 8 pages, contains the wording "send for complete catalog" indicating this is a brief version of a more comprehensive publication. Cover is yellow.

undated, with red-on-red cover, believed to be 1911-12

Catalog published by The Kennebec Journal Press of Augusta, Maine, consisting of 32 pages.

undated brown on tan (two versions) 1913-14 (same design as above)

Two catalogs with identical information, one published by Griffith-Stillings Press of Boston, Massachusetts, the other by Walker Lith. & Pub. Co. of Boston. Each consists of 32 pages.

green on yellow 1915 (same design as above)

Catalog published by Coe-Printwell Advertising Service of Portland, Maine, consisting of 32 pages.

1916 Catalog published by The University Press, Cambridge, Massachusetts, consisting of 32 pages. Cover is mint green on light gray.

1917 Catalog consisting of 32 pages; cover contains use of multiple colors and shades, appearing like a painting or postcard.

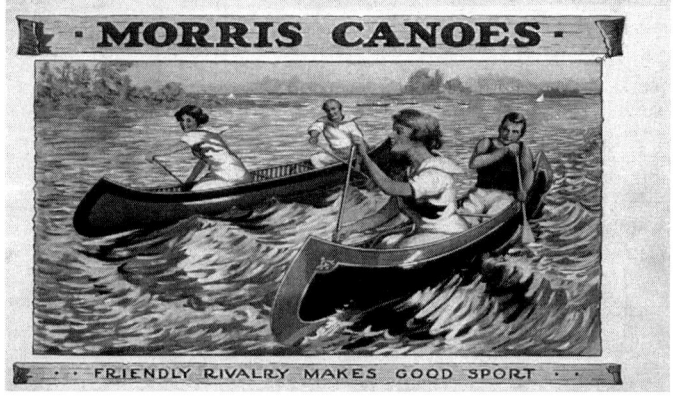

1919 Catalog consisting of 32 pages; cover with action-packed image is highly-colored.

Models, Types, and Styles

The Morris Models

Indian (c.1890-c.1899)

This canoe is built in style and model similar to the Bark Canoe. It makes a fine, speedy paddler for Hunting and Fishing. Built in one grade only, they are constructed in a similar manner to all others in this catalog except the seats, which are narrow and mortised into the gunwale in proper places for paddlers at the Bow and Stern. Built 12 to 18 feet in length, at a price of $20 to $32. (1893 B.N. Morris catalog)

If we consider details of the Indian Canoe as described in the 1893 catalog, no examples of this canoe have entered the Morris Database. The canoe was said to be "constructed in a similar manner to all others" in the 1893 catalog. The other boats are described as having hardwood stems and being planked in pine. While the earliest Morris in the database is similar in appearance to the Indian model in the 1893 catalog, its planking and stem are cedar. The stem is splayed, which is the single-most identifiable factor in regard to a Morris canoe, and tapered ribs are fitted into pockets in the inwale-- another Morris-feature.

The early Morris I have described may well be an "improved" version of the Indian model. I hesitate to call it an early version of the Special Indian because it retains some of the primitive elements of the Indian model, in that it lacks seats and decks and its single, delicate thwart was created out of ash with a spoke shave. The centrally-placed thwart bears the only known example of a metal tag with the words "B.N. Morris/Builder/Veazie, ME."

INDIAN MODEL.

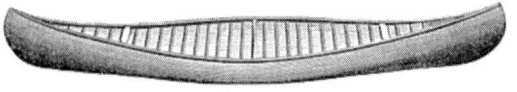

NO. 31, LENGTH, 15 FEET.

In the 1880s, canoe builder Evan Gerrish of nearby Bangor was selling canvas-covered canoes with a metal tag stating "E.H. Gerrish/Maker/Bangor, ME". Similarly-worded tags were used by other builders, although some of them came after Morris had stopped using the "builder tag" and had begun using a decal to identify his work. Additional examples of metal tags with wording similar to the Morris "builder tag" are:

F. Brodbeck/Maker/Boston

C.P. Nutting/Maker/Waltham, Mass

Buck & Packard/Foxcroft ME

Indian Old Town Canoe Co./Builders/ Old Town Maine USA

JR Robertson/Maker/ Auburndale

JH Rushton/Canton, NY

It seems Bert Morris initially chose to follow the example of contemporaries when he began using a metal plate indicating his canoes were produced with the personal, hand-crafted-touch of a specific builder, rather than making it appear they were mass-produced. Hyping the importance of a large factory would come later, with changes due to mechanization and marketing as the twentieth century approached. In the early years of commercial canvas canoe production, attaching the name of a specific man to a canoe appeared to be the way to proceed.

The old Morris canoe mentioned earlier was retrieved from a boathouse in Michigan's Upper Peninsula. Failing a test-paddling due to openings in canvas and planking, she sank-- and would have become part of the lake had rescuers not been at hand. In the magical way that things sometimes happen, the old canoe came into the possession of those who recognized her ribs, her stem, and the name on the metal plate.

Ash thwart with tag reading "B.N. Morris/Builder/Veazie, ME"

Rounded rib-end in rounded inwale pocket of "builder tag" Morris; later Morris canoes have a squared-off rib-top fitting into a squared-off pocket as seen on p. 90.

MORRIS CANOES

The Morris Special Indian Model for Comfort and Safety.

Durability and Excellence of Finish are well-known features in the Morris canoe. We will be pleased to send you a catalogue giving net prices and a full description.

50 State Street,   B. N. MORRIS,   VEAZIE, ME.

1902 advertisement in *Pine Tree Jungles: A Handbook for Sportsmen and Campers in the Maine Woods*

Special Indian (c.1894-1905)

This is a safe family and very popular all-around canoe. In point of stiffness and buoyancy in its size, it cannot be excelled. The lines are most graceful and paddling qualities fine. It makes a fine canoe for experts as well as amateurs, for pleasure paddling or hunting trips. It carries a good weight on slight draft, which is a most important feature in a hunting canoe. I sincerely recommend this model as the right craft for all-around canoeing. Keels are put on to order. 15-18 feet long; priced $40-$42 in first grade and $31-$33 second grade. (1901/1902 catalog)

In the early 1890s, a second Morris model was introduced: a canoe with the familiar heart-shaped decks, thwarts, and seat-frames that are recognizably "Morris". With the addition of mahogany trim tooled like fine cabinetry, the Indian model became a special boat—one that might be viewed as more than a product useful to fishermen and hunters: something that might be enjoyable to paddle, simply for the sake of paddling. The second half of the nineteenth century saw more interest in Nature: parks were incorporated into city-plans; people watched birds, pressed flowers, and read about Nessmuk's adventures paddling the

Adirondacks. However, the difference between the early Morris models lies more in their construction than in their suggested use: in moving from the Indian to the Special Indian, Morris went from creating canoes entirely with hand tools to employing mechanization. In a 1912 article on his company in the *Bangor Daily Commercial,* Bert Morris would explain, "... a high-class article to be sold at a low margin of profit must be standardized and put through in large numbers."

> Canoemen will find it to their interest to examine the descriptive circular and price-list of the canvas canoes manufactured by B. N. Morris, of Veazie, Me. These canoes are remarkable for lightness, stiffness and general durability, and are rapidly displacing the Indian bark canoes. They are light, convenient to transport, easily propelled, and are unexcelled for hunting and fishing. L. W. Ferdinand & Co., of Boston, Mass., are agents for these products.

From the June 6, 1893 *Manufacturer and Builder*

The first dealer to offer B.N. Morris canoes in their catalog was L. W. Ferdinand of Boston. Their 1891 catalog contains an image of the Indian model identical to the image in Morris's 1893 catalog (p. 41).

In their 1898 catalog, the John P. Lovell Arms Company devotes a full page to promoting the Special Indian, saying, "... for safety I shall recommend this model for all purposes where paddling a canoe is desired... This model has been used by hundreds of people in the past four seasons, and in every case has given great pleasure and perfect satisfaction" suggesting a start-date for the Special Indian of 1894.

An 1899 L.W. Ferdinand catalog offers the Morris Indian model and the Special Indian as well. By 1901, the simpler Indian Model no longer appears in Morris catalogs. The Special Indian would be re-named Model A in 1905 and would remain Morris's most popular canoe throughout the history of the company.

Morris's Indian model bridged the gap between the bark canoe and the modern-appearing Special Indian. Correspondence directed to Bert Morris during the 1890s substantiates the fact that both models were available simultaneously. Offering both models not only placed more "Morris product" before the public, it may have helped move the public mind toward acceptance of a modern-looking canvas-covered canoe. The availability of both the "primitive" Indian model and Morris's more "special" version offered the public the options of a traditional-appearing work-craft and one that might be used to impress.

Interestingly, the Special Indian in the Ferdinand catalog is described as having maple decks and ash thwarts and seats, whereas the Special Indian offered in the Morris catalog is trimmed in mahogany. Both are listed as "first grade". Lovell Arms' first-grade Morris is described as having "wedges (decks), seats and thwarts of best mahogany or birds-eye maple."

Three examples of a Morris with a metal tag reading "From/The Morris/Canoe Factory/Veazie, Maine" have been entered in the Morris Database. These early Special Indian models are mahogany-trimmed canoes with the same overall appearance common to the Morris, but aspects of their construction suggest they pre-date all but the very early Morris with the "B.N. Morris/Builder" tag. The word "factory" on the tag of this Special Indian reflects the use of mechanization in the process of building Morris canoes, which appears to have begun in the early 1890s and may have been ramped-up following the Morris brothers' Columbian Exposition experience in 1893. An advertisement by Morris agent Lovell Arms (p.66) suggests a beginning-date of 1894 for the Special Indian.

Morris's use of the metal nameplate places these canoes at a time prior to implementation of the decal to fasten their name to their product. Decals were invented in the mid-1890s and may have seemed a modern—and perhaps less-expensive—alternative to use of a metal nameplate. For more than twenty years, Morris canoes would leave the factory with a decal on their bow deck or bow coaming. Until the first of these metal-plate-canoes came into the database, it was believed Morris never marked their canoes with the Morris name using anything other than a decal.

The woodworking on the "Factory tag" canoes exhibits more finesse than on canoes considered to be "later". Seat frames and thwarts are essentially the same as on later canoes, but with finer edge-work: routing on the thwart-edges gives the central portion a raised appearance, and seat frames have a similar routing on three sides. One Factory tag Morris has finely-tooled mahogany thwarts and seats, but decks are ash—a hardwood not commonly seen on first grade canoes.

A special-order Morris in the collection of the Adirondack Museum at Blue Mountain Lake has similar woodworking details but is without the Factory tag. All Morris canoes have sculpted decks, nicely-shaped thwarts, and seat-frames with champhering; the additional woodworking details seen on the Factory tag canoes may have seemed an unnecessary step as demand for Morris canoes increased through the 1890s.

At least one canoe with the Factory tag contains a reinforcement in bow and stern that seems experimental, given the fact that it doesn't exist in other Morris canoes. It possesses a secondary level to the stem inside the canoe—another piece that follows the curve of the end and extends onto the floor of the canoe for a short distance, on top of the stem that is the recognizable, splayed Morris stem—like an outside stem, only on the inside. This appears to have been an effort to reinforce the ends of the canoe.

The older Morris with the metal tag stating "B.N. Morris/Builder/Veazie, ME" also has reinforced ends, but this was accomplished in a different manner. Instead of a "stepped" inside-stem, the "Builder tag" Morris has double outside stems, with one outside stem under the canvas and one over the top of the canvas. It would seem Bert Morris worked at the problem of reinforcing the ends of his canoes, eventually adding a third pair of cant ribs, high into the nose, in the early 20th century.

At some point between 1895 and 1900, Morris began placing a decal on the heart-shaped short deck or the bow coaming of their canoes. The Special Indian model would become the Model A in approximately 1905.

Double outside stems on "builder tag" Morris

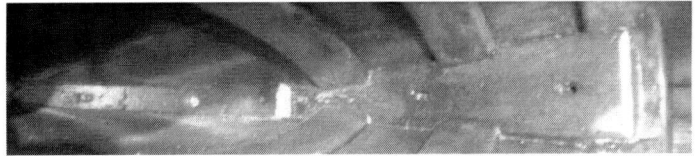

Early version of Special Indian with a "stepped" stem

Morris thwart with "Factory tag" (courtesy Dave Barnes and Martin Bender)

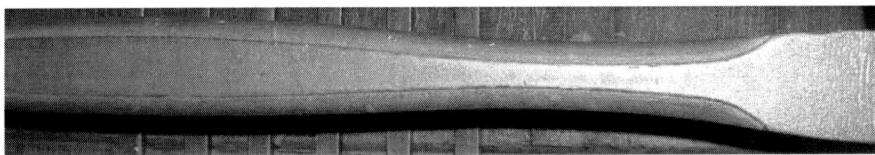

Mahogany thwart on early Special Indian model—note extra woodworking detail

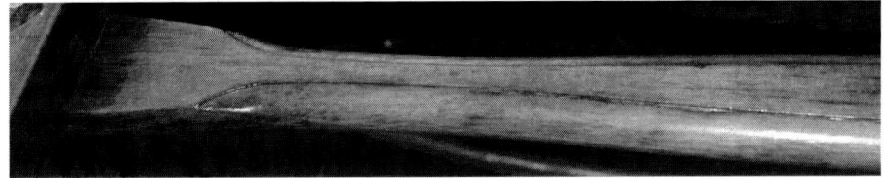

Birds-eye maple thwart on early Special Indian built with a slat seat (p.77). This canoe is missing its center thwart and may have originally had a "Factory tag". The extra woodworking details found on thwarts and seats of Factory tag canoes appear to have been discontinued by Morris in the late 1890s. (courtesy Michael Grace)

Detail of seat-frame on early Special Indian model

Indian Extra Beam (1898-1905)
(referred to as Indian Model Lake Canoe in 1903 catalog)

An extra wide canoe [that] can be fitted with oars, making a fine, safe rowing and paddling canoe. It is a very fine proportioned craft, graceful in lines and beautifully and durably finished. I recommend this craft as safe for children. Built only in first grade. Model built in 12, 16, 17, and 18 foot sizes; priced from $35-$43.   (1901/1902 catalog)

From 1903 catalog: *This model makes a very fine row boat when fitted for rowing, which costs $10 extra, fitted with first class rowing equipment.*

The catalog image of the Special Indian Extra Beam was used by Morris beginning in 1898 as a logo on stationery and receipts, and is incorporated into the logo of the Wooden Canoe Heritage Association.

Because of its extra width, the Extra Beam has a wider angle at bow and stern and requires a wider deck, which is the easiest way to differentiate this model from the Special Indian (unless the canoe is 12 or 13 feet long; the narrower Special Indian wasn't made in these sizes, so any 12 or 13 foot Morris is an Extra Beam or a Model B). Measuring with a protractor, the angle of the short deck on the Special Indian (and later Model A) is 8 degrees as opposed to 12 degrees on the Extra Beam (and Model B). The Indian Extra Beam (a.k.a. Lake Model) would become the Morris Model B in approximately 1905.

Also known as the Special Indian Extra Beam, the Lake Model would be renamed Model B in about 1905. (Image from 1903 catalog, courtesy Daniel Miller)

Model For Speed (1901-1905)

I can furnish an Indian model, No. 92, 16 ft., No. 93, 17 ft., No. 94, 18 ft., beam 30 inches, depth 11 inches. This model has very little tumble home, has good lines for speed, is very graceful in appearance, and has given perfect satisfaction, as a speedy canoe. It is quite safe with proper handling, but is built for speed only. (1901/1902 catalog)

From the 1903 catalog: *No. 93, 94 and 95 lengths, 16, 17 and 18 feet, beam 30 inches, depth 11 inches, price and style of finish same as high grade Special Indian Model. This model has very little tumble home, has good lines for speed, is very graceful in appearance and has given perfect satisfaction as a speedy canoe. It is quite safe with proper handling, but is built for speed rather than safety.*

Interestingly, the single Morris receipt known to exist is for a 17 foot No. 94 that was shipped in 1903.

Special Indian Model for Hunting (1903)

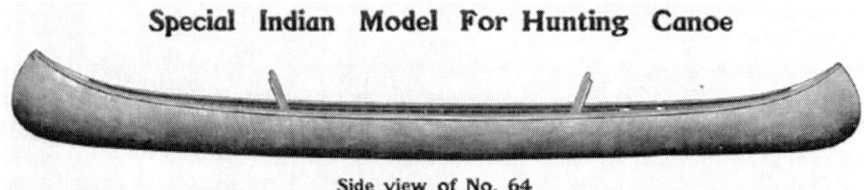

Image from the 1903 Morris catalog (courtesy Daniel Miller)

Essentially the second-grade Special Indian:
These canoes are built for use where extra fine finish is not required. Although they are not highly finished, they are well finished and constructed most thoroughly. The materials used in them are the same as in the highest grade, with the exception of the seats, decks and braces, which are made of oak. Seats are cane filled.

Note that none of the aspects of the Hunting Model are described as "second grade"; Morris uses the same hull in the creation of this model as with the higher-priced models, but the hardwood trim isn't mahogany. This sets the stage for splitting-off the lesser-priced canoe into the Veazie Company and advertising the B.N. Morris canoe as top grade only.

The Shift to "All One Grade"

> FOR BEAUTY, COMFORT, SAFETY AND DURABILITY
> MORRIS CANOES ARE PRE-EMINENT
> ONE QUALITY ONLY, THE BEST

"First grade" and "second grade" initially referred to significant differences in hull construction, finishing materials, and trim woods. The 1893 Morris catalog states "a part of the difference in the cost is in the finish, and part in the choice of the material". In describing the second grade canoe, Morris is "... not quite so particular in selecting the material as in the best grade..." , and they are even less particular in selecting material for a third grade canoe, "... though it must be free from knots and sap." The 1898 Lovell Arms catalog and 1901 Morris catalog describe second grade canoes planked in pine. Lovell Arms mentions first grade trim as "finest mahogany or bird's eye maple." It wasn't unusual for Morris agents who produced their own catalogs to offer canoes with trim-options not seen in Morris catalogs.

By 1901, the Extra Beam version of the Morris Special Indian (the canoe that would eventually become Model B) is offered only in first grade, while the more popular Special Indian model remains in two grades. With the 1903 catalog, both the Special Indian and the wider Extra Beam version are available only as first grade canoes. Morris presents their second-grade canoe as a separate model, describing the other Special Indian models as "the regular High Grade Morris Canoe".

The 1901 catalog lists two seat-options for the Morris first grade Special Indian: a cane-filled seat and a seat upholstered in an imitation leather called Moroccoline, which Morris recommends over the cane. The second grade canoe has slatted seats, and trim is oak or birch. As there are no known Morris catalogs from the years between 1893 and 1901, it may be assumed these seat-versions were available prior to the turn of the century as well. One database-canoe exists with the upholstered seat. The mahogany frame of this seat is identical to cane-filled Morris seats, but without holes drilled for cane and with the central space filled by a leather-upholstered insert. The horse-hair-filled insert is constructed on a separate frame, in the manner of an upholstered dining room chair. This seat might have seemed a comfortable cushion when dry, but obviously didn't work out as a long-term plan. By 1903, the seats of Morris canoes were cane-filled, with no other options.

By 1903, the Special Indian and Indian Extra Beam are offered only in first grade, and a separate Special Indian Model for Hunting is advertised as being constructed of the same materials as the other canoes but with oak trim instead of mahogany. By this time, hull distinctions have disappeared: there is only one grade of hull construction. All are referred to as "the regular High Grade Morris Canoe", the ribs and planking of "the finest quality of cedar", the rails of "clear, straight grained spruce". The term "second grade" has been dropped altogether. 1905 sees the last advertisement for the Morris Special Indian.

Last known mention of the Special Indian Model, in 1905 *Recreation's Advertiser*

Morris agent Abercrombie & Fitch offered canoes in two grades until 1909, when a change was made. Although presumably built by Morris, the Morris name isn't mentioned in their catalogs until that year. In 1909, A&F began to hype their canoes as being all one grade, trimmed in mahogany, and produced "...with the skill of the best canoe builder in the world, Morris."

Slat seat on Morris believed to be pre-1900. Seat frames are maple and slats are spruce. Short seat-frame members are attached under long frame pieces with half-lap joint and screws; slats are attached with escutcheon pins. Decks and thwarts on this 17' canoe are bird's eye maple. (courtesy Michael Grace)

Hair-filled seat covered in "Moroccoline", which Morris recommended as the better of two options for a first grade canoe in 1901. (courtesy Robert Bragg)

Model A (1905-1920)

Model A, is for all-round use, and will be found efficient, safe, staunch and comfortable, principally due to the flat floor, full rounded sides, and remarkable surface bearing. Its dimensions are moderate and pleasing in lines, and from its first appearance on the market up to this day, all users have only the highest appreciation. This model is built with two styles of ends; the Special, or so-called Torpedo ends, and the Standard Ends. (1919 catalog)

"Special Ends" were offered as an option toward the end of Morris production, on the Model A only. In 1916, Morris charged an extra $3 for this option, but by 1917, Special Ends were a choice without extra charge. They added greater recurve to the ends of a canoe, giving it an appearance popular at the time with canoes designed for recreational use and courting. The popularity of Special Ends in the later Morris years has led to the impression that the Morris profile became more elongated or "torpedoed" over time, but the straighter, "Regular Ends", used by Morris since the early 1890s, were offered until the factory's demise.

Model B (1905-1920)

Model B, which is a later development, has been very much appreciated by those who desire a canoe with greater capacity, for family use. It has been on the market a number of years, with a steady increase in demand. Its lines in general are very pleasing, and its paddling qualities are exceptional, considering its dimensions. It is also a very fine canoe to equip for rowing. (1919 catalog)

Model B is the designation given the Indian Extra Beam (also referred to as the Lake Model), and is the canoe most likely to be fitted for rowing. It can be difficult to distinguish one Morris model from the other using pictures, and measurements listed in catalogs may not coincide with an existing canoe one hundred years after it was built. However, the wider B Model has a greater angle in its ends and requires a wider deck. Measuring with a protractor, the short deck on model A is 8 degrees and model B is 12 degrees.

Model C (1905-1920)

Model C, carries about the same dimensions as Model A, except that it has less tumble-home and sharper lines fore and aft. It is a fairly speedy canoe. (1919 catalog)

Known to be a bit "tender", Morris cautions prospective buyers that this model "is fairly speedy but not recommended for safety."

Model D (1905-1920)

Model D is a design with more freeboard and less tumble-home. Has quite a flat bottom, and is quite seaworthy. its paddling qualities in quick water are excellent, and it is unequalled as an open sailing canoe. Its principal uses are hunting and cruising. (1919 Catalog)

Although it is suggested that this model be used for sailing, the more-popular Model B appears to be the Morris most commonly fitted with sails. The design of Model D suggests it may have been favored by hunters wishing to bring moose out of the bush.

Tuscarora (1916-1920)

A model designed especially for racing, and is without a doubt a fast canoe. It is built in two lengths, 17 and 18 feet. To obtain lightness it is fitted with light, tough spruce wales, seats, braces and decks. It is also furnished without keel or floor rack, unless ordered (no charge). (1919 catalog)

Morris Tuscarora as depicted in the 1919 catalog (courtesy *The Complete Wood Boat and Canoe Manufacturers Catalog Collection* edited by Daniel Miller and Benson Gray

The Tuscarora is the only Morris model displayed in the catalogs with the curved short deck that gradually replaced the heart-shaped deck between the years 1913 and 1917; the heart is no longer seen on Morris canoes beginning sometime in 1917 to the end of production. Although the curved short deck was the only one used by Morris in the years that the Tuscarora was built, older images of short-decked canoes continued to be used in catalogs until the end. Without scrutinizing the text to determine that the Tuscarora was trimmed in spruce and only built in 17 and 18 foot sizes, the 1916, 1917 and 1919 catalogs might give the impression that any Morris with the curved short deck is a Tuscarora; however, few canoes of this model may have been built, and as of 2015 only one confirmed Tuscarora has been reported to the Morris Database.

Sponson Canoe, Sailing Canoe

Sponsons and sail rigging could be added to any of the Morris models, although the model most likely to be fitted in this manner was the Model B (or the earlier Indian Extra Beam or Lake Model) due to its additional width and intended use on lakes and wide rivers.

Sponsons are essentially air chambers attached to either side of a canoe, making it difficult to capsize. They are constructed of the same cedar as the canoe's hull and are canvas-covered. The top of the sponsons, referred to as "decks" in Morris catalogs, could be covered either in canvas or mahogany. Morris's sponson canoes had their own Style categories:

Sponson Style 1: The canoe has short decks, without coaming; decks of sponsons canvassed, filled, painted, and varnished; outwale finished with a half-round bead of mahogany and topwale finished with a flat mahogany strip.

Sponson Style 2: Decks on canoe are 24 inch mahogany; decks of sponsons are canvas, which is painted and filled like the rest of the canoe (but could be a different color); coaming all around the interior as with

Style G non-sponsoned canoe (p. 84).

Sponson Style 3: Decks on canoe are 24 inch mahogany; decks of sponsons are mahogany; coaming all around the interior; outside stems.

Sailing canoes are seen with and without sponsons. Morris **sail rigging** consists of a sail, mast and boom, mast seat (or mast bar) and step, and leeboards. Factory-fitted sailing Morrises do not have a rudder. See page 111 for images of Morris sail rigging and Paddle Strokes 6 for resource information.

Morris 16556 is a 17', Model B, Style 3 sponson canoe that originally cost $85.80 in 1919.
(courtesy Ryan Hough)

Motor Boat (1910-unknown)

Canvas covered, cedar ribs and planking, mahogany wales, decks and transom. All materials of the best grade and constructed in the strongest and most durable manner consistent with comparative lightness. (1911 catalog)

Image from the 1911 Morris catalog (courtesy *The Complete Wood Boat and Canoe Manufacturer Catalog Collection* edited by Daniel Miller and Benson Gray)

While seemingly unrelated to the Indian canoe, the Morris Motor Boat was an attempt to compete that fell by the wayside with the popularity of the outboard motor. The number of years this boat was manufactured is unknown; it doesn't appear in the 1916, 1917 or 1919 Morris catalogs but could have been offered in a separate flyer. An expensive craft, its price with motor ranged from $225 to $500-- or $5625 to $12,500 in 2014 dollars. Per report of Morris descendants, a Morris Motor Boat was kept at the Morris cabin on Pushaw Lake. As of this writing, none of these boats has come into the Morris Database.

Double End Canvas Covered Rowing Canoe (1917-1920)

An ideal craft for safety, durability and speed. It is built light (which is a point commonly requested) but thoroughly constructed, and you may be assured of Morris quality. These canoes are finished in open wale construction and outside stems. have substantial keel, brass bang plates and galvanized row-locks. Stock colors dark green and gray. (1917 catalog)

Although not a direct descendant of the Indian Model canoe, this offering was created to fill a niche in the market, and appears related to boats built by Charles Morris and used at his camp on Pushaw Lake. It was available in 15 and 16 foot lengths. Unlike the typical Morris canoe, this boat's stem is narrow and constructed of hardwood, and it was offered only with open gunwales. A single example has entered the Morris database. The serial number plate on the inwale informs us these boats were in a different serial numbering system from that used for the Special Indian and A-D Models.

15 foot Morris Double End Canvas Covered Rowing Canoe; this boat has Morris decal version 3 (courtesy George Fatula)

Morris Outboard Motor Canoe (1919-1920)

A square stern canoe designed especially for detachable or outboard motors. Open gunwale construction, thoroughly braced to withstand vibration. (1919 catalog)

In appearance, this boat has the lines of a typical Morris canoe with Special Ends and Outside Stems at the bow, but with a transom at the stern. The canoe was "thoroughly braced" with plank seats and was available only in 17 and 18 foot lengths. The Outboard Motor Canoe may have been available as early as 1918, but there are no known catalogs to confirm this. No boat of this type has entered the Morris Database and it is likely not many were sold before the factory ceased production.

Morris Types

Type 1: Spruce gunwales, mahogany seat frames, braces (thwarts), short decks. Spruce grate (floor rack). Keel.

Type 2: Spruce inwales, stained. Mahogany top and outwales. 24" mahogany decks, flag socket, painter ring, mahogany seat frames and braces (thwarts), spruce grate (floor rack), keel.

Type 3: as with Type2, with the addition of oak outside stems

Short-decked Morrises could also have outside stems, but this wasn't a designated "type". Addition of Special Ends or Special (D-shaped) Outwales to any Morris canoe also didn't generate an assigned "type".

Morris Styles

Styles (1917-1920) Assigning letters to the different gunwale treatments on Morris canoes happened in the final years of production. The three gunwale-versions (Open, Closed, and Closed with Special Outwales) had been offered at least since 1910, but had never been assigned a letter designation. The other style described by Morris involves the amount of coaming that could be used in trimming-out a long-decked canoe.

Style H: Standard Morris closed gunwale

Style J: Standard Morris open gunwale

Style K: Closed gunwale with Special Outwale (D-shaped, mahogany)

Style G: This option applies to long-decked canoes. Instead of coaming that only "finishes the circle of the deck", this coaming "is continuous entirely around inside, projecting slightly above the topwale"

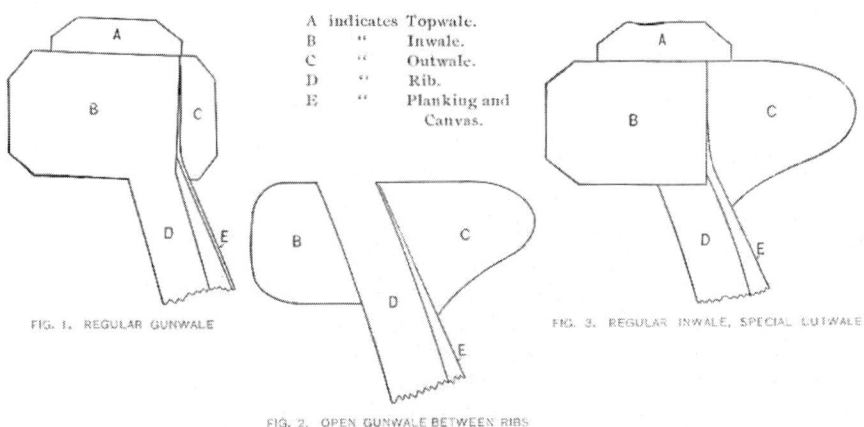

Gunwale options as depicted in the Morris catalogs (courtesy *The Historic Wood Boat and Canoe Manufacturer Catalog Collection* edited by Daniel Miller and Benson Gray). Outwales ("C") on figures 2 and 3 are referred to as "D-shaped" and were always mahogany. Outwale in figure 1 was spruce but could be upgraded to mahogany. Note bevels on inwales, top caps, and figure 1 outwale—they are not simply flat pieces but are fashioned with finesse.

Morris Style G (described p.83); note wide sitting thwarts (courtesy Robert Bliss)

Serial number plate on inwale of Morris Double End Canvas Covered Rowing Canoe pictured p.81 (courtesy George Fatula)

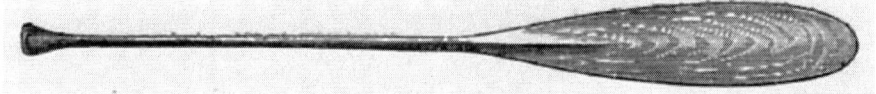

Paddle Strokes 6

Tracking the Journey...

This chapter relies upon Morris catalogs found in *The Historic Wood Canoe and Boat Manufacturer Catalog Collection* edited by Daniel Miller and Benson Gray, on canoes entered into the Morris Database since 2007, and on occasional bits of ephemera that have appeared in the years since the "rediscovery" of the Morris canoe. In 2001, WCHA member Paul Miller bought a group of letters written to Morris that were offered on eBay. Dating to the 1890s, the letters contain requests for catalogs and discuss product offerings. A June 1898 letter from the Capitol Electric Company inquires about the price of a canoe "...illustrated in an inset that we find in one of your 1893 catalogues... the illustration number of this canoe is No. 62 but the model that our customer wants is No. 63 with a list price of $40.00, as this is an old catalogue we thought that there might have been some change in the price... ." The 1893 catalog that is known to exist contains no boat of any kind wIth numbering that high, but in the 1901 and subsequent catalogs, number 63 is the Special Indian. I wrote about this in *Wooden Canoe* Issue 148, Vol. 31, no. 4 (2008), as it was the first indication that the older Indian Model and the Special Indian existed simultaneously.

A group of nine similar letters given to Rollin Thurlow is discussed in his article *More B.N. Morris Canoe History*, Wooden Canoe Issue 50, Vol. 15, no. 1 (1992). One of these letters is addressed to "B.N. Morris and Bro.", indicating knowledge that Charlie Morris was part of the business.

I have also found letters to Morris on eBay. Three envelopes dated 1894 were offered because of their stamps; one envelope includes a letter, addressed to B.N. Morris, asking, "what is the lightest canoe you make for carrying 2 people and traps, say 500# in all?" Bert's notation at the bottom of the letter-- "40, no length mentioned"—is presumably a cue for a secretary's formal reply. Another of my eBay-finds is dated June 18, 1898 and contains a query regarding a second-hand canoe—the first suggestion I've seen that Morris offered used canoes, and has me wondering if people traded-in an old canoe or "traded up" to something longer or fancier. In the case of this letter, the notation "a nice one for 30" is Bert's reply. Letters such as this may have been part of an estate sale, perhaps as long ago as Margaret Morris's death in 1950.

Additional Resources

The Historic Trade Catalog Collection in the Baker Library at Harvard University.

Bradshaw, Todd, *Canoe Rig: The Essence and the Art*, *Sailpower for Antique and Traditional Canoes*, Woodenboat Books, 2000.

Bradshaw, Todd, *Replicating a 1908 Morris Lateen Sail*, WCHA Forums, December 10, 2011, may be found at:
http://forums.wcha.org/showthread.php?8557-Replicating-a-1908-Morris-Lateen-Sail

7

ANATOMY OF THE MORRIS CANOE

My two old canoes are works of art, embodying the feeling of all canoemen for rivers and lakes and the wild country they were meant to traverse. They were made in the old tradition when there was time and the love of the work itself. – Sigurd F. Olson

The Morris is possibly the easiest of the older canvas canoes to identify, due to its distinctive stem. The stem is the part that forms the outside edges of a wood and canvas canoe, creating the curve of bow and stern. The inside-face of the stem may be seen extending onto the floor of the canoe, at each end. With nearly every wood and canvas canoe, the stem consists of a narrow piece of hardwood an inch or so wide. With a Morris-built canoe, however, the stem looks rather like a beaver's tail: it grows gradually to a width of about three inches, with a squared-off end that appears to "bite" the first full rib on the floor of the canoe at each end. This is referred to as a **splayed stem**. A few other canoe builders use a stem that widens, but the Morris stem is distinctively different, with a few exceptions such as the Kennebec-Morris "hybrid" (p.202) and the Rhinelander, which was based upon the Morris. Unlike other canoe-builders of his day who constructed stems with a hardwood, Bert Morris chose to construct his stems using **cedar**. Modern reproductions of Morris canoes may also have this distinctive feature.

Explaining the reasoning behind this wide cedar stem, Bert Morris states, "stems are of selected material, steam bent to mold, and spreading on the inside to get the strong support of the ribs. Our method of attaching the ribs to the stems is a decided improvement over the usual method, and is a feature that renders the canoe more rigid, and capable of withstanding the hardest kind of usage."

When the stem is examined, it's easily seen that the splay firmly holds the first full rib, and **cant ribs** that extend up into the bow and stern fit into pockets in the sides of the stem in addition to being held in inwale pockets.

Typical Morris stem: splayed and cedar

Stem on this 1946 Rhinelander is ash, not cedar

Brass (or occasionally copper) **stem bands** at the bow and stern protect the ends of the canoe and are sometimes referred to as **bang plates**. The stem band on a Morris extends only ¾ inch over the canoe's nose, barely touching the edge of the deck. They are fastened with copper

rivets that extend through the stem. The canoe's keel tapers down to nothing to meet the stem band. If the canoe is fitted with **outside stems**, stem bands are typically screwed on, but the cedar stem of the canoe is riveted in place beneath the outside stem. With outside stems, the keel is butt-jointed against the outside stem to make a continuous, flush surface, and the stem band runs across the junction of stem and keel and protects it. Stem bands running from bow to stern, the full length of the keel, could be ordered as an option on a Morris canoe, and stem banding could be affixed to rub rails.

stem band affixed to outside stem and keel with flathead screws

The hull and ribs of Morris canoes are cedar. **Ribs** are 3/8 inch thick; ribs on most other canoes are 5/16. The catalog description of the 1893 Indian model states that the ribs are 3/8 inch thick—so it seems they were made this way since Morris began commercial production. Ribs on Morris canoes are tapered and have beveled edges. Morris initially used white Maine cedar in building hulls, but used red cedar from the West when price and availability made better business sense.

Gunwales (pronounced "gunnels") form the upper edge of a canoe and are sometimes referred to as "the rails". Morris began building canoes prior to the development of the open gunwale, which came about shortly after the turn of the twentieth century. With an open gunwale canoe, the ribs stand full-thickness between an inwale and an outwale. **Closed gunwales** consist of three elements: an inwale, an outwale, and a top cap. The majority of Morris canoes have closed gunwales like the bark canoes upon which they are based; however, Morris employed a construction technique which, while more difficult to accomplish, appears stronger than other closed-gunwale canoes.

Traditionally, canoes with closed gunwales required that rib tops be thinned to fit the closed rail system, thus weakening the ends of the ribs. Morris recognized the importance of maintaining rib-strength, and constructed canoes without removing wood from the rib tips. The ribs of a Morris canoe settle neatly into little pockets in the inwale, in a manner similar to the joinery of fine furniture. This technique provided a closed gunwale canoe that did not compromise rib-strength and might not be as susceptible to rot as those that were thinned to fit the closed rail system. Thus, Morris canoes have **pocketed ribs**.

Morris with missing outwale and planking, showing inwale with ribs fitting into pockets

It has been suggested that Morris may have created these pockets by using a circular drill bit such as a forstner to make holes in a board, which was then cut down the middle to create inwales with semi-circles to hold the rib-tops. Needless to say, the restoration of a Morris canoe needing new inwales can be a daunting project.

Inwales, outwales, and top-cap of a standard Morris canoe are made of spruce, but upgrades were available. If mahogany was desired, Morris offered the option of a sculpted D-shaped **"Special Outwale"** as well as mahogany in a less expensive, flattened strip of wood. All elements of the rails could be made of mahogany, or the inwale might be spruce and the outwale and top-cap mahogany.

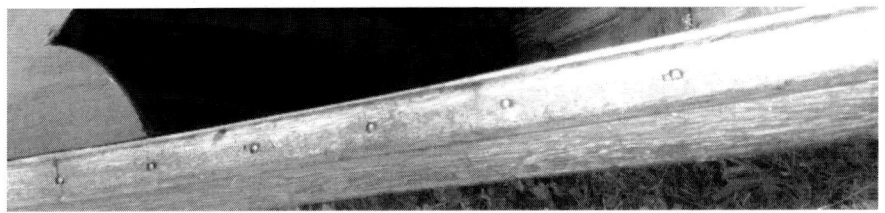

looking downward at the D-shaped Special Outwale

Open gunwales were developed in approximately 1905. Morris possibly began offering them as early as other builders but none show up in the database until after 1910. With an open gunwale, the rib is sandwiched between the inwale and outwale, leaving an opening between the ribs that permits any water that collected inside the boat to be easily dumped out. As well as being more practical, the open gunwale is easier to build than closed-- especially considering the pocketed-rib system of the Morris.

Because the heavy, D-shaped mahogany outwales used in constructing an open gunwale Morris added to the expense of building the canoe, open gunwales were offered by Morris as an option for which the customer paid an additional charge. As the public grew to understand the advantage of open gunwales, they became standard with most manufacturers. However, throughout the life of his company, Bert Morris continued to offer open gunwales only as an option. Perhaps he was proud of the Morris contribution to canoe construction and believed his closed gunwales were as strong as open gunwales. He may have preferred the look of a closed gunwale canoe: the straight, unbroken line of the gunwale having more eye-appeal than the staccato interruptions of the open wale.

In addition to inwales and outwales of solid mahogany, the open-wale Morris has a delicate trim-piece on top of the rails at bow and stern, beginning at the nose and tapering to end about a foot beyond the deck. This provides a suggestion of being closed-railed in the area of the decks, where the eyes of paddlers tend to linger. Morris may have felt this helped customers accept the concept of the new-fangled open gunwale—or it may simply have been a cabinet-maker's touch. The Kennebec Company employed a similar trim-piece on their open wale canoes.

Most Morris canoes are trimmed in mahogany: it seems that decks, **thwarts**, and **seat frames** in first-grade Morris boats were constructed of mahogany from the beginning of Morris's commercial production. A Morris canoe trimmed in any other wood species is either a special-order canoe, a canoe ordered from a Morris agent's catalog (such as Abercrombie & Fitch), a model of lesser grade, or a Veazie canoe (discussed in Chapter 9). Seat frames and thwarts are usually constructed using the same wood species as the decks.

The 1893 Indian model is described as having "sitting thwarts" that are mortised into the inwales. The boats Morris used in the Columbian Exhibition had "cane woven thwarts for paddling seats". In the 1901 catalog, Morris offers a seat with a mahogany frame in their first grade canoe, much like those used throughout their 20th century production, but with a central area cushioned with horse hair and covered with imitation leather, or "Moroccoline". Slat-seats were offered with the grade two canoe. By 1903, all Morris seats have an insert of cane, woven in the 7-step method like a dining-room chair.

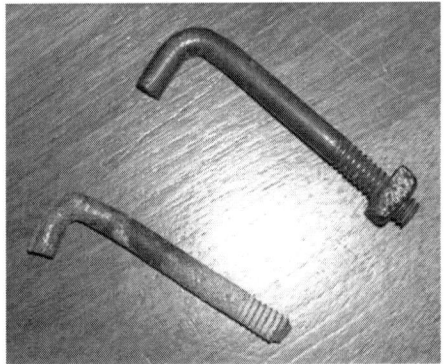

Morris seat hanger bolts

With a closed-gunwale Morris, seats and thwarts are hung from the inwale with an L-shaped bolt. The short end of the L is then covered with the top-cap of the gunwale. Hexagonal nuts are used on the underside of seats and thwarts to secure them. The middle thwart on canoes over 16 feet long is held with wing nuts so that it might be easily removed, allowing more room for gear and passengers; this is presumably the reason why many 17 and 18 foot Morrises are missing their center thwart. With both open and closed wale Morrises, the bow seat is secured to the inwales, as is the front rail of the stern seat. The stern seat's rear rail is lowered, with a 3/8 inch diameter cylindrical copper spacer ¾ inch long, or square wooden spacer, covering the bolt.

Top cap of gunwale is removed, exposing ends of bolts used to hang the seats.

Brass spacer covers bolt on a closed gunwale Morris

Wooden spacer on open wale Morris; this type was also used on closed wale canoes, appearing on canoes of Morris's later period (courtesy Michael Grace)

Morris also refers to his thwarts as **braces**, as they help to hold (brace) the canoe's shape. Typically, canoes that are 12, 13, and 15 feet in length have only one thwart; 16 footers have two thwarts; 17, 18, and 20 foot canoes have three thwarts, with the middle one removable via wing nuts; however, the 17 foot Veazie canoe (discussed in Chapter 9) was sold without a middle thwart.

Standard Morris thwart

Three different styles of short deck were used on Morris canoes: **a heart shaped deck**, a shallow **concave curved deck**, and the concave curved deck with a central circular opening (referred to as "the **keyhole deck**") seen on the Veazie Canoe discussed Chapter 9. Morris refers to the short deck as a **brest hook** in his later catalogs. While a number of builders used a heart-shaped deck, the Morris heart is finely sculpted, appearing to rise slightly in the center. The curved deck (which gradually replaced the heart) fits the hand well and is not as prone to cracking up the center as is the heart. The keyhole deck is essentially the curve with a circular cut-out in its middle. The Morris curved deck appears to have been developed first for the Veazie canoe and migrated to the B.N. Morris models due to its practicality.

Typical Morris Short Decks

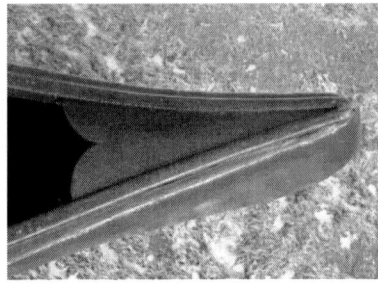

Heart-shaped deck on canoe with D-shaped outwales

Curved deck

Veazie "keyhole" deck

It should be noted that B.N. Morris re-used some of their catalog images even if changes were made in the canoe. The Tuscarora model, which was introduced in 1916, is the only canoe in a Morris catalog shown as having the curved deck, giving the impression that a Morris canoe with a curved deck is a Tuscarora. Re-taking pictures for catalogs might not have seemed worthwhile, and it probably didn't cross Bert's mind that folks a hundred years later might be concerned as to which model Morris canoe they were paddling. He does make it clear in the catalog that the Tuscarora is a narrow, lightweight canoe built for racing and is trimmed in spruce rather than mahogany. Our database of over 300 canoes suggests the first curved decks appeared on B.N. Morris canoes in 1914 (and on the Veazie prior to that), and the heart-shaped deck was phased-out completely in 1917. The curved deck is offered as a replacement, beginning with the 1917 Morris catalog.

The 1893 Morris catalog states "If decks are required from eighteen to twenty-four inches long add three dollars...". And thus we know that the earliest version of the Morris canoe didn't have the classic Morris heart-shaped deck.

Morris canoes with long decks also exist. By 1917, decks could be ordered in lengths up to 52 inches at each end, the most common being 24 inches. Long decks on Morris canoes consist of four elements. Two separate triangular deck-pieces meet at the center to create the deck. This is topped with a tapered cover-plank to hide the seam. A steam-bent piece, called **coaming**, trims the inside edge of the deck. The deck's central plank (sometimes referred to as the "king plank") might contain a diamond-shaped pennant holder.

Morris with long decks, showing right and left sections, tapered king plank with name of owner on brass tag, pennant holder, and coaming with original decal. (courtesy Craig Kitchen)

The long decks on Morris canoes are supported by a framework of at least two pieces, as the mahogany itself is only ¼ inch thick. The length of the deck dictates the design of the framework that holds it. On occasion, a short deck has been discovered under a canoe's long deck, suggesting it began life as a short-decked canoe, morphing from a Type 1 to Type 2 or 3.

Framework of Morris 24" deck (courtesy Jerry Karbon)

Curved short deck found under long deck of Morris canoe

From 1916 until the end of production, Morris offered the option of **Special Ends** on the Model A canoe: stems at bow and stern curve dramatically outward in a manner sometimes referred to as "torpedo" or "recurved stems". This look was popularized by the canoe liveries along Boston's Charles River, where beautifully painted, long-decked canoes with sweeping ends became fashionable. The style evolved from canoes built for racing, their extended stems efficiently cutting through waters.

Outside stems consist of trimming the bow and stern with hardwood, bent to the curvature of the outside edge. Outside stems are decorative and also help protect the ends of a canoe from over-zealous paddling near docks and snags in a river. A canoe designed for outside stems has differences in construction. Note that the outwales and rub rails on *Belle* (p.101) extend onto the outside stem; the keel is butt-jointed to it.

Rub rails are an option offered in the later Morris catalogs. They consist of a hardwood strip that stretches from bow to stern several inches below the gunwales on either side of the canoe. Rub rails are more commonly seen on livery canoes, as they help protect the boat from the bumps it might get in the course of paddling canoe-choked areas and canoe-renters without much paddling experience. Rub rails also suggest the need for at least a two-tone paint-job, which was fashionable in courting canoe arenas.

Ken Kelly's Belle Isle Morris has Special Ends, outside stems, and rub rails

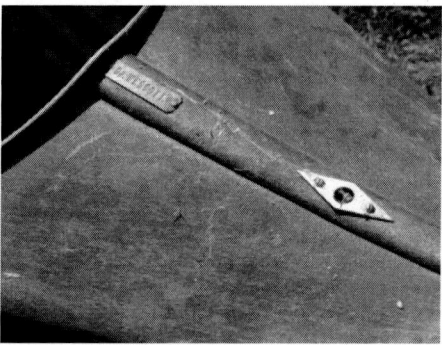

Diamond-shaped Morris pennant holder; owner's name on rectangular plate near coaming may not have originated at the factory (courtesy Craig Kitchen)

Pair of optional Morris eagle-topped flagstaffs
(courtesy Joseph Brown)

Morris #15288 with 48" decks and optional wide sitting thwarts (courtesy Robert Bliss)

Most Morris canoes have a full-length hardwood keel attached at every rib with #8 bronze screws. Morris states that his "regular" keel is " ½ inch on the shoe, ¾ inch in depth, 7/8 inch on base, and tapers at ends to the width of the stem band." Signs of a **keel** having been **attached at every rib** is one of the diagnostic elements of a Morris, as most other builders attached the keel at every other rib. The wide shoe keel more commonly seen on the canoes of Canadian builders is offered as an option in Morris catalogs for an additional price.

Morris canoes were sold with a **floor rack** made of spruce, held in place by a toggle made from a piece of stem band. The option of **half ribs**, or short, auxiliary ribs stationed between the regular ribs, made a floor rack unnecessary. Interestingly, a Morris floor rack found in a 17 foot Model B canoe has "17 B" penciled on the underside.

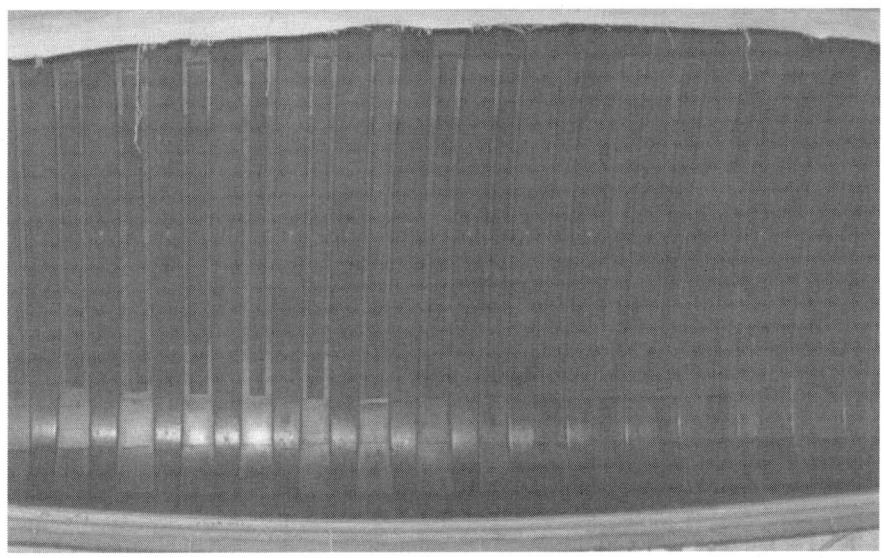

Half ribs are stationed between full ribs in this Morris Molitor; note that screws are placed in every full rib, except those ribs that were recently replaced. Keel was yet to be reinstalled.

Image showing toggle holding floor rack in place;
stem band was used to create Morris toggles.
(courtesy Brad Cornelius)

A **painter ring**, or piece of hardware for attaching a rope ("painter") to a canoe, came with certain Morris Types or could be added to a canoe at additional cost. The factory-installed painter ring on a Morris appears to be something one could find in a hardware store today, only they were nickel plated brass. Morris painter rings may be found on the floor of the canoe, attached to the bow stem. If the canoe has a serial number plate on the stem, the painter ring is centered above it.

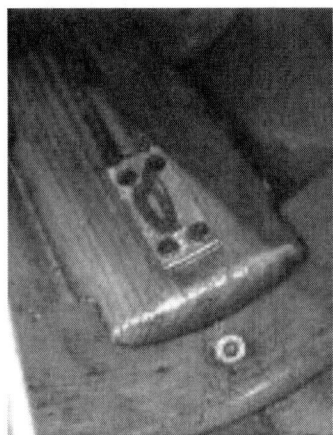

Painter ring on stem

A **serial number** may be found on a brass plate: either an oval on left inwale, near the first full rib, secured with two brass escutcheon pins; or, a rectangle with rounded corners, located on the bow stem, secured with four brass escutcheon pins. The plate is also known to occasionally be placed on the side of the bow seat-frame in long decked canoes. The significance of a serial number in determining the age of a Morris is discussed in Chapter 12.

Oval serial number plate on left inwale

Rectangular serial number plate on bow stem

It is rare to find the Morris name on a factory-installed metal plate, but two versions are known. A metal tag reading "B.N. Morris/Builder/Veazie ME" may be the earliest version, followed by one with the words "From/The Morris/Canoe Factory/Veazie Maine". A Morris canoe might have a metal medallion or a decal bearing the name of the retailer through which it was sold, such as Abercrombie & Fitch or Folsom Arms. The canoe's serial number may be engraved on a dealer's tag. A Morris might also have the tag of a canoe livery and a livery number.

Folsom Arms brass medallion on Morris 3746, c. 1906 (courtesy Michael Cyr)

Decal of Chicago Morris agent Von Lengerke & Antoine on coaming of long-decked Morris (courtesy Craig Kitchen)

B.N. Morris Decals

With the invention of the **decal** in the mid-1890s, Morris discontinued use of the metal name-tag. Four versions of a B.N. Morris decal and one version of a Veazie Canoe Company decal are known to exist. Exactly when the metal name-plates were discontinued and the first version of the decal was employed likely happened in the second half of the 1890s.

Three decal-versions have been found on the bow deck of short-decked Morris canoes.

Version 1 on Morris without signs of a serial number (courtesy Norm Sims)

Version 1

B.N. MORRIS
CANVAS CANOES ROW BOATS
AND EQUIPMENTS
VEAZIE, MAINE

Version 1 has been found on four canoes in the Morris database that never had a serial number; it likely dates from the late 1890s.

Decal on Morris number 70, which dates to 1900 (courtesy Ian Conk)

Version 2

B.N. MORRIS
BUILDER
CANVAS, PADDLEING (sic) & ROWING
CANOES.
VEAZIE, MAINE.

Version 2 is found on canoes with very low serial numbers through 9XXX. Of the database canoes with this decal, 70 is the lowest serial number and 9240 the highest, suggesting a beginning-date for Version 2 of about 1900 and discontinuation of the decal sometime in 1912. Note that "paddling" is misspelled.

Decal version 3 on Morris 13809 (courtesy Greg O'Brien)

Version 3

B.N. MORRIS
BUILDER
CANVAS, PADDLING & MOTOR
CANOES
VEAZIE, MAINE

Version 3 is found on canoes with serial numbers 10XXX and above; 10090 is the lowest serial number in the database with this decal. Morris came out with a motor boat in 1910 and was promoting it heavily in 1911-13.

One decal version has been found on Morris canoes with long decks, placed centrally on the bow coaming (see image p. 98). Wording is the same as that used on one of the metal name-plates used by Morris prior to decals.

B.N. MORRIS
BUILDER
VEAZIE, MAINE

Morris may have marked their "equipments" with a decal, but very few examples have come forth. Existing decals have been found on these items from other canoe manufacturers, so it is reasonable to assume Morris did the same.

Morris decal version 2 on lee board bracket

Morris decal versions 2 and 3 and the coaming decal have been reproduced and are available from the WCHA Store. It is generally advised that if any traces of an original decal are present, they be maintained rather than removed and replaced by a new one.

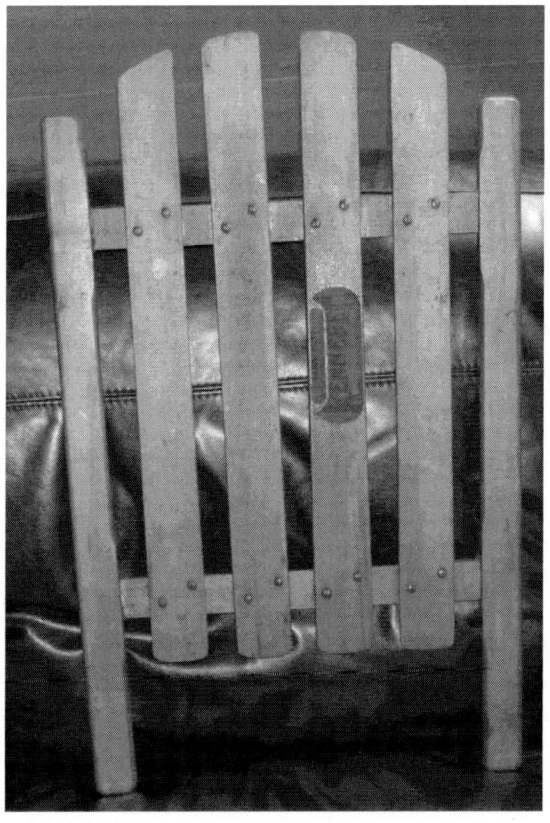

Morris and Kennebec offered similar backrests and canoe chairs in their catalogs, leading to speculation that they shared the same supplier or, if constructed within the factory, that Kennebec backrests and chairs were built by former Morris employees. This backrest has a Wannamaker Sporting Goods decal as well as a Kennebec decal; without the decal, it appears identical to a backrest offered by Morris.

Open gunwale Morris owned and restored by Dave McDaniel. Note short decorative gunwale caps, heavy D-shaped outwales, typical Morris seat with 7-step cane pattern, and beautifully sculpted heart-shaped deck. Seats are attached with round-head slotted screws on an open gunwale Morris. (courtesy David McDaniel)

The Canoe of Greatest Value   **MORRIS**

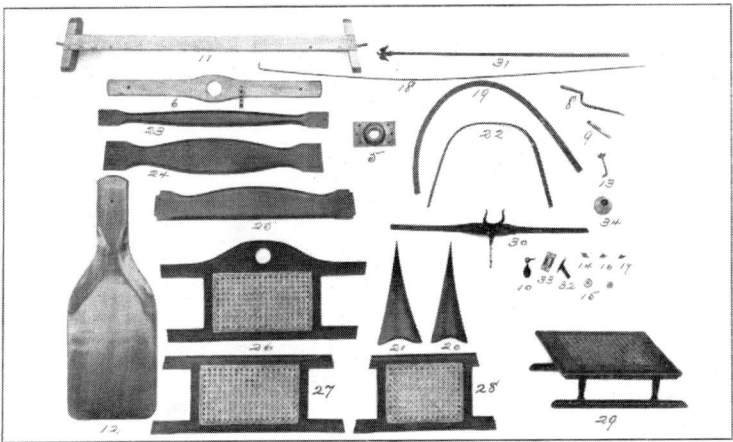

CANOES   *The Canoe of Originality*

Repair Parts and Accessories
ORDER BY NUMBER (See Opposite Page)

No.			No.		
1	Sail	$3.50	21	Brest hook of Mahogany for Type 1. Model B	$0.50
2	Mast with Block	1.75	22	Coaming for Type 2 or 3, 24" deck	.35
3	Boom with Jaw	1.75	23	Brace 2⅛" regular	.35
4	Gaff	1.00	24	Brace 5" regular	.60
5	Mast step	.50	25	Brace 5" straight one side	.60
6	Mast bar with block	1.00	26	Mast seat, caned	2.00
7	Sheet and Halyards (Ropes)	.50	27	Bow seat	1.25
8	Jaw for boom	.50	28	Stern seat	1.00
9	Jam cleats (2)	.50	29	Rowing-stool	1.50
10	Polished brass block	.50	30	Rowlocks with blocks and screws	3.00
11	Leeboard bar	3.50	31	Flagstaff with eagle tip	.75
12	Leeboard blade—each	1.50	32	Flagstaff socket (2)	.50
13	Clamp hook with nut—each	.25	33	Painter loop with screws	.25
14	Wing nut for clamp hook	.10	34	Drip cups for double paddles	.40
15	Washer for clamp hook	.05	35	Floor rack	1.25
16	Wing nut for leeboard blade	.10	36	Setting pole	1.75
17	Wing nut for Middle braces	.05	37	Ambroid Cement, quick, durable, prepaid	.30
18	Brass bang plate (specify Type)	.75	38	Repair kit, for patching and retouching (mention color desired) 75c, prepaid.	.90
19	Outside stem ready to put on	.80			
20	Brest hook of Mahogany for Type 1. Models A-C-D-E	.50			

Images of Morris parts that were available in the 1917-19 catalogs. Note the curved deck (brest hook) is offered as replacement for the heart. (courtesy *The Historic Wood Boat and Canoe Manufacturer Catalog Collection* edited by Daniel Miller and Benson Gray)

Morris Paint Colors

Standard Morris colors consist of red and several shades of green, although a customer could choose any other color. Records from the company dating from 1910-1913 show they used Sherwin-Williams paints.

The following colors are offered in existing Morris catalogs:
1901: Indian red, light and dark olive, light and dark green
1903: deep red, light and dark olive, light, medium and dark green
1910-1915: red, light and dark olive, light, medium and dark green
1916: red, olive, light, medium and dark green, gray
1917-1919: red, light, medium and dark green, gray

A paint chip card included with a letter from Bert Morris dated 1905 lists examples of the following as Morris Standard Colors (which I will do my best to describe, as this book is in black and white):

Indian Red (a deep burgundy, nearly red-brown)

Cart Red (a bright burgundy)

C.P. Green, Dark (an almost black-green)

C.P. Green, Light (medium "hunter" or "forest" green)

Sage Green (a dark olive)

Light Olive

N.H. Green (green with a bit of yellow)

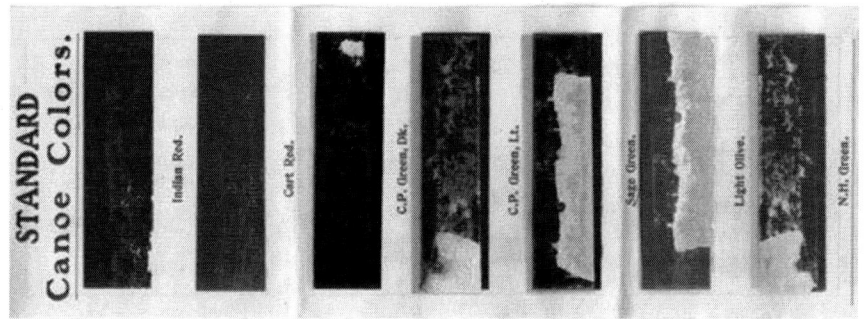

Morris paint colors offered in 1905, shown mainly to demonstrate its condition, as images in this book appear in black and white.

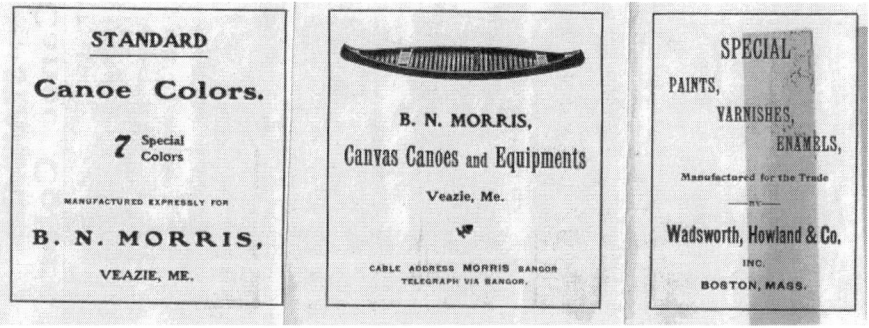

Reverse of paint chips, revealing that Morris bought their paint from Wadsworth, Howland and Company of Boston in 1905. The letter accompanying this item, to Rhodes Bros. Co., is typewritten (by someone with initials SER) and signed with Bert's signature stamp (in contrast, a Morris receipt from 1903 contains Bert's hand-written signature). The letter to Rhodes Bros. involves the purchase of a number of specially-built canoes with long decks and mahogany rails. Rhodes Bros. Co. managed Rhodes-on-the-Pawtuxet, an historic recreational complex in Cranston, Rhode Island.

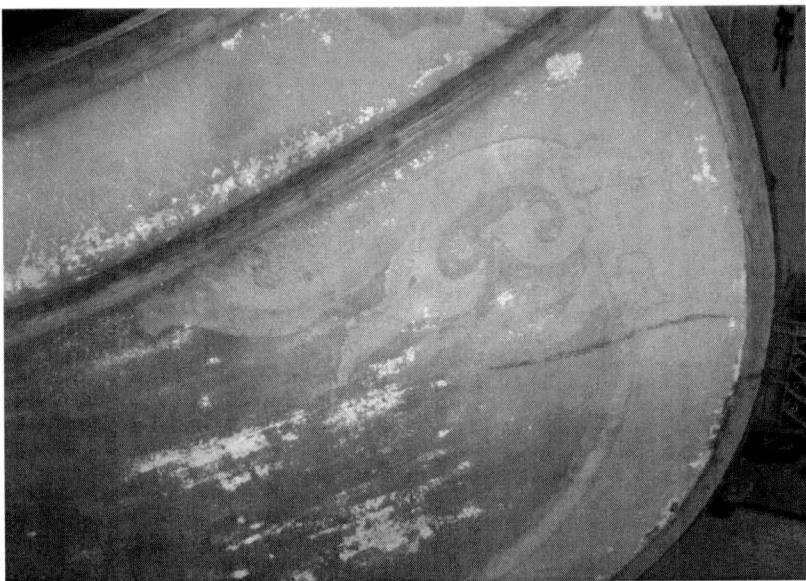

Remains of a fancy paint job on a Morris Belle Isle Molitor

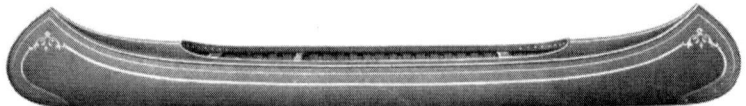

Plate 2   Model A, Type Three, Style G, 38 inch Decks

The above illustrates canoe finished in two colors. Striping and scroll in gold leaf or color. Price, as above illustrated, decorated in gold leaf, $75.00. Decorated in color in place of gold leaf, $72.00. Has wide braces in place of the cane seats.

Fancy paint-job suggested in the 1919 Morris catalog

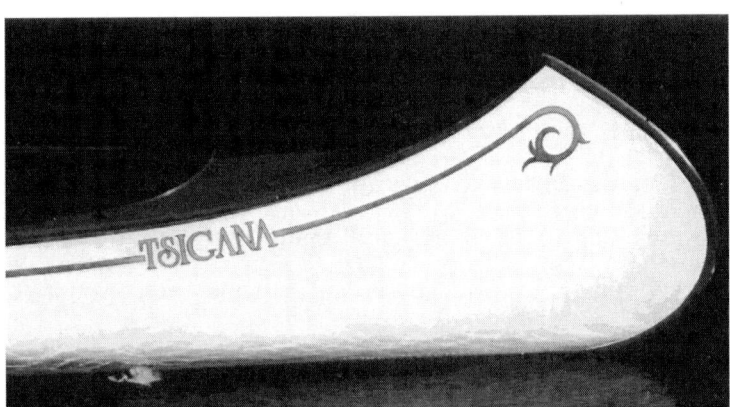

Gold leaf design on restored Morris (courtesy Scottie Baker)

Getting Down to Brass Tacks...

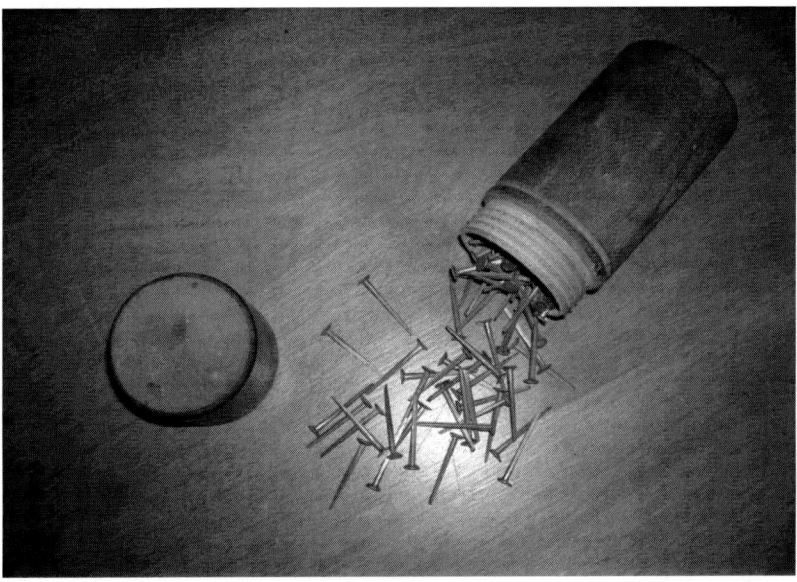

Brass tacks from the house on Flagg Street in Veazie, which were collected into a wooden container with screw-on lid. It is unknown whether these tacks were used in the canoe-building process, but I like imagining they were handled by Charlie and Bert.

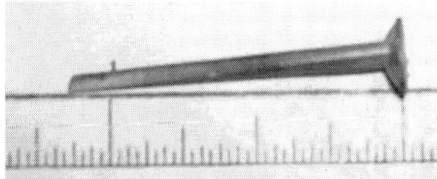

Up-close and personal of brass tack, showing it to be 1 1/8 inches long. Container of tacks was found in the shop located in the ell of the former Morris home in Veazie by its current owner.

8

THE CANOES OF BELLE ISLE

O, come with me in my light canoe...O, come with me and be my love.
-- America Singing: Nineteenth Century Song Sheets

The Island Calls

Once known as Hog Island, where pigs ran freely and fattened without falling prey to anyone or anything, Belle Isle sits in the middle of the Detroit River, with the city of Detroit on one side and Windsor, Ontario, on the other. Turning Belle Isle into a show place may have seemed a bold move in 1883 when Detroit's citizens voted for improvements to the island that would offer families the quiet of the countryside within the expanding city. As a result of the vote, the city engaged landscape architect Frederick Law Olmstead, noted for designing New York City's Central Park, to work on the Belle Isle project.

Islands hold a romantic lure, and Belle Isle was designed to be especially alluring. Swampy areas were filled and replaced with a system of tree-lined canals bisected by ornate arched bridges. Rolling green expanses of grass were planted, making sites for games and picnicking. It was a landscape dotted with fountains, pavilions, and covered bandstands, connected by walkways rimmed with flower beds. In 1889, a bridge was built which connected Belle Isle to the Detroit mainland. As public interest in Belle Isle rose, the city added a casino, arboretum, aquarium, zoo, and pony rides. After the turn of the twentieth century, the city dredged out two more lakes on the island, Takoma and Okonoka, and extended the canals, which became choked with canoes on warm summer weekends.

E.A. Davis ran a boathouse on Belle Isle in 1889, and Murdoch McCauley is listed in city directories as a livery owner in 1894. At no more than two feet deep, paddling posed little danger to non-swimmers with only the threat of getting wet should the canoe capsize.

Postcard showing lapstrake rowboats on Belle Isle

The first canoes to ply the waters of Belle Isle were all-wood lapstrake vessels of simple grace and beauty. These rowboats and canoes were far different from the ones an enterprising Charles Molitor began selling from a corner of his father's Detroit grocery in 1906. Like many who are born into a family business, Charles had worked beside his father from childhood. The Morris dealership was his; however, it was in his father's store. By the 1890s, canoes had appeared on the canals that were very much like wood and canvas canoes of the twentieth century. After 1906, many of these canoes may have come from the canoe concession at Molitor's Grocery, some possibly filling the liveries already on the island.

As a canoe dealer, Charles Molitor was no doubt aware of a growing public interest in the canoe as a recreational vessel. Canoes were being sold for the purpose of simply paddling around, rather than the traditional uses of fishing and hunting. The canals of Belle Isle were filled with canoes, as canoeing had become a popular summer pastime; in 1910 an additional canoeing area, Sylvan Creek, was completed to accommodate the need for more room on the water. By 1910, Charles Molitor, then age 26, had been a dealer in B.N. Morris canoes for four years. Pictures of Belle Isle from this era show canoes that appear to be those of B.N. Morris, and C.J. Molitor was the sole agent for Morris in Detroit.

Like other young entrepreneurs, Molitor might have desired to be out on his own, in a place where his wares had greater visibility and where the canoes he sold were perhaps already in use. Molitor also may have felt pressure from Detroit-area boat builders such as the Detroit Boat Company, whose factory was situated a short distance from the Belle Isle Bridge. A prominent spot across from the island would appear to be the ideal place for setting up his own shop, with a fleet of his canoes in the livery across the water, on the island.

Charles Molitor's Morris canoes were perfect for recreational use. Unlike the canoe typically used by a hunting and fishing guide, the Morris had beautifully upswept ends, gracefully curved stems, and could be ordered with long decks of gleaming mahogany instead of the simple heart-shaped deck—and have seat frames, thwarts, and gunwales to match.

On Belle Isle, boys in crisp white shirts assisted renters into fully outfitted and beautifully trimmed canoes. As a Morris agent, Charles Molitor would have known that Bert Morris could build the sort of canoe that would turn heads and entice a young man desirous of wooing his lady to choose a canoe from C.J. Molitor's Belle Isle Livery.

Opening in May of 1906, Electric Park hugged the shoreline on the Detroit side of the river opposite Belle Isle. Detroit's first large-scale amusement park, with its entrance near the Belle Isle Bridge, Electric Park was purported to be one of the largest such parks in the world. Three streetcar lines terminated at the bridge which served as a grand entrance to Belle Isle. The previous year, the Detroit Department of Parks and Boulevards began bus service to the island. The Belle Isle Bridge was one of Detroit's busiest intersections, where-- especially on summer weekends in 1910-- it may have seemed like all the city was taking advantage of the amusements that Electric Park and Belle Isle had to offer.

Belle Isle's main canal in its heyday

In 1910, Charles Molitor entered the Joy Amusement Company, a penny arcade east of the bridge connecting Detroit proper to Belle Isle. It stretched from a walkway just inside the amusement park to the water. Penny arcades of the day were filled with the whirl and ding of multiple Mutoscopes and machines designed to test physical strength, forecast the future, and provide winnings. Perhaps Charles Molitor considered the building's proximity to the bridge, or the ferry that was available for those wanting to begin a canoeing experience with a trip on a different sort of vessel. Whatever his reasons, Molitor's Canoe House was established at the rear of the building, where windows held views of the river and the island beyond.

Electric Park from the Detroit River, c. 1906 (courtesy Wayne State University)

A Morris for Courting

The canoe B.N. Morris built for C.J. Molitor's livery had it all: long decks sporting flagstaff sockets, mahogany rub rails extending the length of the boat on either side, heavy D-shaped mahogany outwales, outside stems, and sturdy mahogany thwarts in addition to caned seats. This canoe was as fashionable as some on Boston's Charles River.

It may not be wicked to go canoeing on the Charles River with young women on Sunday, but we continue to be reminded that it is frequently perilous....The canoeist arrested for kissing his sweetheart at Riverside was fined $20. At that rate it is estimated that over a million dollars' worth of kisses are exchanged at that popular canoeing resort every fine Saturday night and Sunday. -- The Boston Herald, August 24, 1903

In the early-twentieth century, formal courtship rituals of the Victorian Age were still in practice. The use of the canoe in courtship began in the late 1800s, when at least a dozen canoe-building businesses were established along the banks of the Charles River in Massachusetts, several of them offering canoes for rent. The Charles was a river of easy paddling and quiet beauty—the perfect romantic backdrop for showing off canoes that, by 1910, were works of art. The Morris was easily adapted to the social and recreational purposes that drove the evolution of the canoe from sporting tool to courting tool, and there were a half-dozen agents in the Boston area selling canoes to liveries and to those wishing to paddle their own canoe.

Image from a Morris catalog c.1915 (courtesy *The Historic Wood Boat and Canoe Manufacturer Collection* edited by Benson Gray and Daniel Miller)

The boats in Charles Molitor's livery—eighteen feet long, with three-foot bow decks and two-foot stern decks— may very well have set the standard for the liveries on Belle Isle. The fore and aft decks displayed pennants on foot-long poles. For wooing a lady on a moonless night, there were carbide spotlights, like those used on Ford's Model T, attached to the bow decks of some of the canoes. Paddlers could rent a Victrola, complete with morning glory horn, and rugs for the floor, backrests that propped against the thwarts, and a supply of pillows—some emblazoned with the Belle Isle name. Tasseled roping, draped from bow to stern along the outside of the gunwales, not only added to the canoe's decoration but deflected the bumps of other canoes in the canals of Belle Isle, which became crowded as the second decade of the century progressed.

Canoe Supplies of all Kinds   Second-Hand Canoes Bought and Sold

CHAS J. MOLITOR
The Canoe Man

Sole Agent for
MORRIS HIGH GRADE CANOES   Canoe Storage

Canoe House
1472 Jefferson Ave., Above Belle Isle Bridge
DETROIT

Advertisement from 1911 Detroit Directory

Forces of Change

Belle Isle continued to draw people through the second decade of the twentieth century. In 1914, city officials decided to turn all of the city's riverfront into parkland, with picnic areas and bandstands along the

Detroit River. This plan had barely gotten off the ground with the construction of a streetcar station at the entrance of the Belle Isle Bridge as the only completed step, when a new "craze" caught people's attention. Perhaps the impact of the automobile should have been more obvious to people in Motor City than those living elsewhere. The city was moving outward, and the automobile took people even farther-- to natural rivers and quiet places not found in the crowded inner city-- and a canoe could be strapped onto a car to make the journey.

In addition to renting out canoes, Charles Molitor, as "The Canoe Man," continued to sell B.N. Morris canoes from his shop at the rear of the penny arcade. He also bought and sold used canoes and rented storage space to those wanting to keep their own canoe on the island. Morris agents consisted mainly of dealers who sold a variety of sporting goods and canoes built by several companies— the Old Town Canoe Company, J.H. Rushton, and others. Charles Molitor may have been the only Morris agent who dealt exclusively in B.N. Morris canoes and accessories. It appears that Bert Morris appreciated the business he received over the years from his Detroit agent; he honored the Belle Isle canoes with a picture on page 5 of his 1917, and subsequent, catalogs.

Canoeing is a summertime affair, however, and Detroit is in Michigan with several months of cold weather. Raised at his father's side in the family grocery, Charles Molitor was above all else a businessman; in 1916 he opened Molitor Screen and Storm Sash, a company engaged in the manufacture of windows. While this new business venture lacked the glamour of canoes and the excitement of amusement parks, it did meet a human need in a growing city.

A man with a keen business eye takes stock of changes that might impact business. The amusement park's atmosphere was changing and aging. Its ill-maintained rides, which charged the blood of the young, began to offer thrills for reasons other than fun. While the situation on the island with the canoe livery remained as before, the changes began to add up.

Page 5 of 1917 Morris catalog, showing canoes on Belle Isle (courtesy *The Complete Wood Boat and Canoe Manufacturer Collection* edited by Daniel Miller and Benson Gray)

In 1911, Palace Gardens, a dance hall near the penny arcade building, burned to the ground, and in 1915 the Belle Isle Bridge itself caught fire. There had always been watchmen stationed on the bridge, ready to extinguish small fires started by cigars and cigarettes carelessly tossed onto the creosote blocks that paved the bridge. On a day in April, hot coals used for asphalt work on the island spilled from a steel cart onto the bridge, leaving a trail of fire. The steel and wooden bridge built in 1889 was a total loss. C.J. Molitor's Canoe House, just beyond the bridge, was untouched. The fire with the greatest impact on Charles Molitor's business occurred in December of 1919, when eight of the nine buildings comprising the B.N. Morris factory were destroyed.

While the "Roaring Twenties" saw the end of Bert Morris's factory, the canoes of Belle Isle continued to be a popular summer pastime. In 1920, material was added to the west end of the island, increasing its size to nearly 985 acres. In 1921, Charles Molitor became a dealer for Old Town Canoe of Old Town, Maine, and ordered thirty-one new livery canoes, which were shipped from the factory June 1. Appearing much the same as those that had come from the Morris factory, the canoes Old Town built for Charles Molitor were eighteen feet long, with three-foot bow decks and two-foot stern decks, outside stems, rub rails, gleaming mahogany, and closed gunwales with pocketed ribs. These canoes—referred to as the Molitor Model on Old Town build records—were the last canoes to be ordered for the livery of Charles Molitor. Although Old Town could accomplish fancy designs on its canoes, these final boats ordered for the livery were a solid-colored dark green, blue, orange, black, brown and red, without further embellishment. That February, another fire at Electric Park destroyed its largest concession, the Coliseum and Pier. In 1922, Charles Molitor left the canoe dealership and livery behind to focus full-time on the Molitor Screen and Storm Sash Company. He was a businessman and factory owner, and this product carried his own name.

The Morris Molitor Legacy

Throughout most of the 1920s, Molitor models-- built under the Carleton name as well as that of Old Town-- were shipped all over the United States. Although never a catalog offering, the Old Town Molitor was available to anyone who wanted a fancy courting-type canoe. By 1922, they were constructed with open gunwales and in 17 as well as 18 foot lengths. Old Town retired the original Molitor model in the late 1920s.

After the Second World War, canoes may have seemed to old-timers like Charles Molitor to be caricatures of the canoes that had won their youthful attention; however, C.J. Molitor might have understood the business decisions behind craft made of aluminum and fiberglass, which fit a modern image of the canoe and needs of the people. Charles Molitor had had his day, at a time when a person could run their hand the length of a three-foot deck of book-matched mahogany and know the boat was among the best on the island.

On May 30, 1964, an old canoe with dramatic torpedo stems and mahogany trim was received into the repair shop at Old Town canoe, where canoes by any builder were again made water-worthy. If a canoe was of known manufacture or was tagged with a builder's name, that name would be listed on a detailed record of its repair; if the canoe's builder was unknown, it would be listed according to type, such as "guide style". With its highly recurved stems, the old canoe that entered the shop in 1964 was unusual, generating much attention by Old Town's employees. It was possibly the product of a Charles River builder, many of whom didn't mark their canoes; however, an older employee recognized its type, as Old Town had once made such grand canoes back in the 1920s. The canoe was designated "Molitor style".

It may not have seemed a prudent business decision to offer a high-end courting canoe in the mid-1960s, but the attention generated by the old boat while it sat in the repair shop was impressive. In 1965, Old Town began offering a courting-type canoe based on this repair, and called it "The Molitor". The modern Old Town Molitor is different from the Molitor Old Town offered in the 1920s, appearing more like the work of a Charles River builder rather than C.J. Molitor's tricked-out Morris canoes. Instead of long mahogany decks, the modern Molitor has two twenty-inch, sculpted decks. Where the canoes of Molitor's livery had three thwarts-- the middle one removable via wing nuts-- the modern Old Town Molitor is built with rails so substantial it requires no thwarts at all. Unlike the canoes in Charles Molitor's livery, the modern Molitor is seventeen feet long. It remains Old Town's most expensive canoe.

There is a story, recounted in the discussion forums of the Wooden Canoe Heritage Association website by Benson Gray, of the Gray Family that founded Old Town Canoe. In the 1970s, a young business student asked the manager of Old Town why he continued to list the Molitor in the catalogs when the company sold so few of them. He responded by saying, "some people like to buy a Lamborghini."

Charles Molitor's legacy may appear to be only that of the name Old Town attached to a canoe that was a spin-off of the canoes of Bert and Charles Morris. However, it's a larger story: one of men who took the pulse of a nation and filled a moment in history with a joyous option. It was a time when many of the people of this world had moved beyond personal survival and were privileged to follow their ambitions, and in the fulfillment of dreams may lie the defining-portion of a human life.

Today, Belle Isle is on the National Register of Historic Places, which describes the park's period of significance as 1900 to 1924, only two years beyond the time of C.J. Molitor's canoe business. At more than nine hundred acres, Belle Isle is the largest island park in the United States. The years between 1884 and 1908 saw the development of most of the island's roads, bridges, lakes, shelters, and plantings. Today, it appears much the same as it did when Charles Molitor's livery offered elegant rental canoes, but the canoes are gone and the canals are quiet.

In 1927, Electric Park's amusement centers were condemned by the City of Detroit as eyesores. They were razed in 1928 to make way for a public park, which had originally been suggested in 1914. The area where the penny arcade and Molitor's Canoe House stood is today a grassy area with no sign it was ever anything different. Crossing the bridge to the island, the area that once held the canoe livery is equally devoid of any trace of what once was there.

Charles Molitor was thirty-eight in 1922 when he gave up Molitor's Canoe House, devoting his energies for the next forty-six years to the screen and storm window business. It would be interesting to know whether he conformed to the times and eventually built combination windows of aluminum or vinyl; it is unknown how many homes retain his wares. When he died in 1980 at the age of 96, the Detroit paper referred to him as "The Canoe Man of Belle Isle." It seems his years at Belle Isle defined his life.

Some of the canoes of Belle Isle have survived and been restored to original condition—or better. Belle Isle could one day see a reunion of the Morris, Old Town, and other canoes that once graced the waters of the canoe canals. If you are an old canoe, not only can you go home again, you may do so in style.

The Morris Canoe

Postcard titled "Belle Isle By Night"

Belle Isle today

On February 10, 2014, the State of Michigan made Belle Isle Park its 102nd state park, in an attempt to relieve the City of Detroit from the expense of maintaining the landmark property while it is going through bankruptcy.

Belle Isle Morris, complete with carbide light, Victrola with morning glory horn and many, many pillows. (courtesy Russ Hicks)

Livery tag on coaming of Molitor canoe (courtesy Ken Kelly)

Old Town Molitor, shipped in 1922 to agent Iver Johnson in Boston (courtesy Benson Gray)

Morris Molitor that was once a livery canoe on Belle Isle.

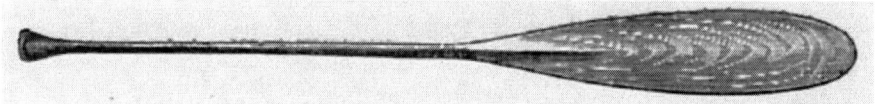

Paddle Strokes 8

Tracking the Journey...

Thanks to Gil Cramer for encouraging me to write the C.J. Molitor story, the original version of which was published in Issue 156 (December 2009) of *Wooden Canoe*. Denis Kallery assisted with research on this project in the Burton Collection of the Detroit Historical Society and at the Maine Historical Society in Portland.

I spent a great deal of time searching for pictures of Charles Molitor, the Molitor grocery, and the Joy Amusement Company, but to no avail. I did, however, find that Charles Joseph Molitor registered for the WWI draft and learned he was of medium height and build, with dark hair and blue eyes.

Detail of C.J. Molitor's WWI draft registration; he had begun making windows by this time

The Morris Canoe

REGISTRAR'S REPORT C 21-1-2?

DESCRIPTION OF REGISTRANT

HEIGHT			BUILD			COLOR OF EYES	COLOR OF HAIR
Tall	Medium	Short	Slender	Medium	Stout		
21	22 ✓	23	24	25 ✓	26	27 Blue	28 Dark

C.J. Molitor's draft registration divulges some of his physical characteristics

SHIPPED: may 24-1923
To: C.J. Molitor
Detroit
Michigan

Canoe No. 77524
Our Order No. 2618
Your Order No.

Via:

Length	18	Half Built	MAR 1
Grade	AA	Model Molitor Completed	
Planking	W.C.	Hull Varnished	
Gunwales	Open Mahogany	Canvassed	
Decks	24" / 30"	Filled	
Thwarts		Stored	
Seats		2nd Filled	
Half Ribs		Stored	
Finish Rails		Railed	Stone
Keel		Fitted	
O.S. Stems		Colored	
Floor Rack		1st Varnished	
Sponsons	H.H.	2nd Varnished	OP
Color	H Green	Stored	

Bilge/Keels, Rub rail with Brass
full length
Rub rail copper " Brass

A final order: Old Town Molitor shipped to C.J. Molitor after he closed the canoe business

135

9

THE VEAZIE CANOE COMPANY

Our object is to produce a canoe that will meet the requirements of the most exacting canoeist for an all-round canoe... at a price within the reach of anyone desirous of owning a canoe ... --Veazie Canoe Company

The 2007 discovery of a catalog for the Veazie Canoe Company of Bangor, Maine, shed light on business aspects of the Morris Company and on an odd type of short deck found on a few of its canoes.

It has been suggested by some who have tried to reconstruct the history of the Morris Company that its original name was " The Veazie Boat and Canoe Company" and that use of the Veazie name went out of existence in the 1880s. If this is true, it seems the Veazie Company re-emerged after the turn of the twentieth century.

The twelve-page, undated catalog Denis Kallery found at the Maine Historical Society in Portland has been scanned and is included in *The Historic Wood Canoe and Boat Manufacturer Catalog Collection* edited by Daniel Miller and Benson Gray. Further research has turned up a 1908 listing of acquisitions by the Providence Public Library, acknowledging receipt of two pamphlets from the Veazie Canoe Company. These pamphlets may well be identical to the catalog that is known to exist; comparison of the Veazie catalog with known B.N. Morris catalogs suggests a pre-1911 date. The catalog was published by Burr Printing of Bangor, which is still in business; however, the Bangor fire of

1911 destroyed company records which might have verified the catalog's date.

The Veazie Canoe Company first shows up in Maine State documents in 1908, when the Annual Reports of Bureau of Taxation and Assessment lists it as valued at $50,000 and taxed at $5.00. Knowing the year Morris created Veazie helps us understand when Morris began promoting the B.N. Morris canoe as "all one grade" and when A through D began to be used in describing their models.

Looking at the canoes themselves places the formation of the Veazie Company circa 1905. Early Veazies can be identified by a distinctive "keyhole" deck. Two canoes with this deck in the Morris database have a serial number plate on their inwale (or tack-holes where one might have been) and only two pairs of cant ribs.

It was with the Veazie that we began considering cant-rib counts in determining the age of Morris canoes in general. WCHA member Paul Miller brought to the attention of the group that his Veazie canoe had only two pairs of cant ribs. We then began inspecting all Morris canoes, and learned that in approximately 1905 a third pair of cant ribs was added to the way Morris hulls were constructed.

Veazie catalog, published by The Thomas W. Burr Printing Co. of Bangor, consists of 12 pages; original is property of the Maine Historical Society. Cover is olive green.

Two canoes by Morris that appear to be twins other than the fact that the upper canoe has outside stems. Upper canoe is a Veazie with keyhole deck, two cant-rib pairs, and evidence of an oval serial number plate on the inwale; lower canoe is Morris 3889, with three cant-rib pairs, shipped c.1906. Note identical planking patterns.

With the creation of the Veazie Company, the B.N. Morris canoe could be advertised as a single grade canoe of the highest quality without suggesting that the company made anything but "the best grade". The Veazie is essentially Morris's second grade canoe, but there is nothing "second grade" about its construction. It was constructed using the same hull as a B.N. Morris, which seems more efficient than to produce separate second-grade hulls of pine or lesser-grade cedar, as Morris did when they offered canoes in two and three grades.

In the Veazie Canoe Company catalog, Morris explains that by cutting out the middleman, they are able to offer a canoe directly to the public at a lower price than other canoes on the market. However, a factory-direct Morris canoe had always been available for less money. Among the interesting Morris-ephemera that has come to light are letters written directly to the factory inquiring about canoe prices, and Bert Morris invariably offers the writer a deal.

The Veazie Company had a purpose, beyond that of offering a factory-direct canoe as stated in the catalog, and it had to do with the competition faced from other builders. By the time Morris created the Veazie Company, B. N. Morris wasn't the only canvas canoe builder selling via agents. Most dealers in sporting goods handled several brands of canoe. Advertisements dated 1911 and 1912 show both The B.N. Morris and the Veazie brand offered by Morris agent Iver Johnson of Boston. With the addition of the Veazie Company, Morris created a dual label system of distribution, putting more Morris-product before the public eye. Old Town Canoe created a similar situation when they bought the Carlton Company in 1910. By the nineteen-teens, Morris had at least fifty agents worldwide, and each could offer the canoes of B.N. Morris and the Veazie Company.

Veazie Wood Species

The hull of a Veazie canoe is the same hull used on a B.N. Morris canoe; any difference between the two canoes involves the species of wood used for trim. The Veazie catalog states that Eastern white cedar is used for hull construction, saying "It is well known that the white cedar of the East is not equaled as a tough light wood, particularly adapted to canoe building." Some twentieth century canoe manufacturers imported red cedar from the West as it became less expensive than Maine cedar of similar size, quantity and quality. Records indicate Maine white and Western red cedar were both in common use by the Old Town Company in 1905-1907. It is reasonable to assume that Morris was hyping use of the local white cedar, although they, too, would be using red as quality Western cedar increasingly became available at lesser cost than white. There is, however, no date at which Morris switched from using white to red cedar for their canoe hulls, as use of white was based upon price and availability.

The standard Veazie canoe was offered with maple or birch decks, thwarts and seat frames; however, the Veazie could be upgraded to an all-mahogany-trimmed, long-decked canoe, fancier than the standard Type 1 B.N. Morris. It's logical to assume the Veazie canoes sold by dealers were trimmed using the less expensive hardwoods and might therefore appear to be "a deal" standing next to the more expensive mahogany-trimmed boat, and a Veazie trimmed in highly-figured maple might appear more attractive to some customers. One truly magnificent Veazie canoe has decks, thwarts, and seat frames of tiger maple.

Some Veazie canoes have a mix of wood species in their trim. One Veazie in the Morris database has a heart-shaped mahogany deck and two have mahogany curved decks. Thwarts and seat frames on these canoes are maple, stained to look like mahogany. Perhaps Morris didn't keep a large supply of maple decks in stock and used whatever was handy.

Veazie Decks

The standard short deck on the Veazie Canoe is of two types. Earlier canoes have the "keyhole" deck: an ogee-type with a large circular center. The keyhole deck occurs on Veazies in the Morris database that had an oval serial number tag on the inwale and some with the rectangle on the stem. Around 1910-1912, Morris stopped making the "keyhole" in the middle of the Veazie deck; with the circle in the middle no longer cut out, the remaining deck became the familiar Morris concave curve. Morris began using this deck-type on the B.N. Morris models in about 1914, presumably because the heart-shape deck was inclined to crack up the center. By 1917, the deck that began on the Veazie canoe is listed in Morris catalogs as a replacement deck for B.N. Morris canoes needing repair, and use of the heart on Morris canoes was abandoned altogether.

"Keyhole" deck

Veazie Serial Numbers

Serial numbers appear on brass tags identical to those used on B.N. Morris canoes. An oval tag may be found on the left inwale, near the first full rib, on earlier Veazies, and a rectangular tag with rounded corners may be found on the stem of later Veazies. Because Veazie canoes were numbered separately from the B.N. Morris, and because far fewer were made, Veazie Canoe Company canoes have low serial numbers. The highest Veazie-number is 1101 and the canoe appears to be post-1915. A similar B. N. Morris would be numbered 12XXX or higher.

Veazie serial number (courtesy Zachary Smith)

The Veazie Decal

The Veazie Canoe Company used an intricate Art Nouveau decal on the bow deck. Unfortunately, only one example has been found and the image isn't clear enough for copying. The decal consists of a shield-shape positioned atop crossed canoe paddles, with the image of a canoe and paddlers on the shield. The shadow of this image is seen on two existing Veazie canoes, in addition to the canoe with actual flaking portions of the decal.

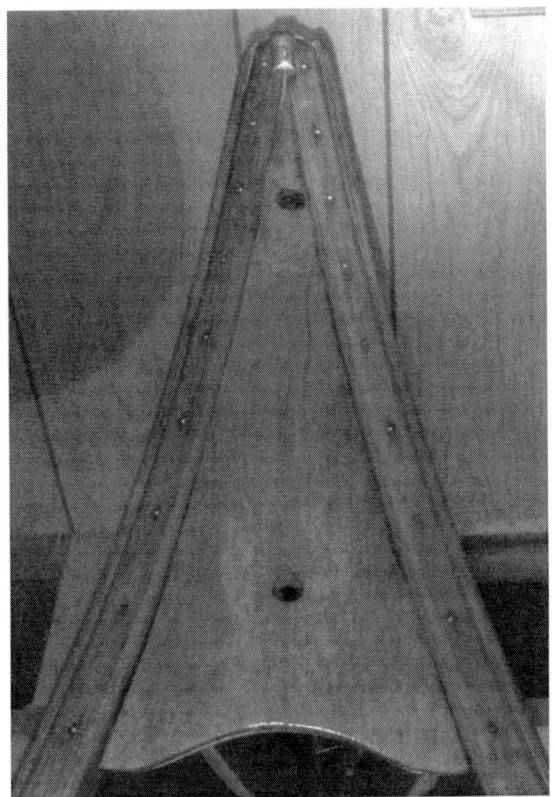

Deck of Veazie 716, showing shadow of decal. Canoe is trimmed in tiger maple and is known to have been purchased in 1913 from Kennedy Bros. in Minneapolis. (courtesy Aaron Moen)

The flaking remains of a decal on Veazie 1032

Canoe Models Offered

The existing catalog for the Veazie Canoe Company lists only a "model A" but it may be assumed any Morris hull could be used, depending on the desire of the buyer.

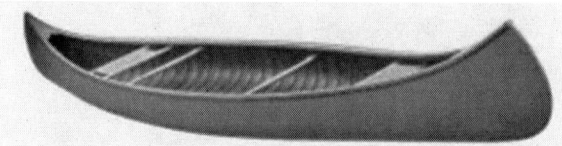

Veazie Canoe, courtesy *The Historic Wood Canoe and Boat Manufacturer Catalog Collection* edited by Daniel Miller and Benson Gray

Dating the Veazie Canoe

Deciding the age of a Veazie canoe is even less precise than the dating of a B.N. Morris; however, the B.N. Morris canoes can be used to determine an age-range for Veazies. If the serial number plate is on the inwale, the canoe is likely 1905-1910; if the serial number plate is on the stem, the canoe is c.1910-1920. If the plate on the stem is oriented with the shorter end parallel to the splay of the stem, it is likely c.1912-1916.

Receipt for fine imposed on Veazie Company by the Internal Revenue Service in 1912

Ad placed by Morris agent Iver Johnson in the *Boston Herald*, dated May 31, 1912, indicating they offered both Morris and Veazie Company canoes (courtesy Howard Herman-Haase)

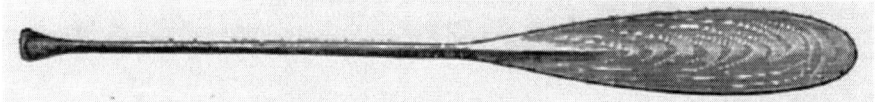

Paddle Strokes 9

Tracking the Journey...

Looking at the Morris database canoes themselves provides the best estimate of the beginnings of the Veazie Company. After Paul Miller pointed out that his Veazie had only two cant rib pairs and it seemed other Morris canoes had three, I began asking for cant rib counts and it became clear that the third pair was added between Morris canoes numbered 2972 and 3013, or circa 1905. As ads for Morris in 1904 still offered the Special Indian and not the all-one-grade Morris models, and there is evidence Veazie canoes existed before the change to three cant rib pairs, it can be assumed the Veazie Company—and the switch to Models A-D—happened circa 1905-06.

There are currently no known Morris catalogs dated between 1903 and 1911, but for the possibility that the Veazie catalog dates from this time, based on some of the text. The 1903 catalog states all Morris canoes are built without keels unless a keel is specifically ordered. By 1911, Morris says "...the keel is regarded generally as a very essential feature, and, finding they are demanded almost exclusively, I am putting a keel on all stock canoes and no allowance made for their omission, and when not required must be finished up from a certain stage of construction."

In considering keels, a description in the Veazie catalog places it somewhere between the 1903 and 1911 Morris catalogs. In the Veazie catalog, Bert Morris states that "in some localities a keel on a canoe is considered unnecessary, while in others it is considered absolutely necessary, and to meet all requirement our stock canoes are finished with and without keels but the prices herein are for a canoe without a keel." It cost $1 more to have a keel installed. It therefore seems possible that the known Veazie catalog may be the same thing described by the Rhode Island library as "pamphlets" in 1908. Page-count is another factor suggesting the Veazie catalog might be considered a pamphlet, as it consists of only 12 pages, although the Veazie Company only had one model to promote and 12 pages may have seemed adequate.

Kathy Klos and Denis Kallery paddle Veazie 1032 on Jag Lake in Wisconsin (courtesy Ferdy Goode)

10

ENDINGS

The older I get, the more clearly I remember things that never happened.
Mark Twain

The evening of Monday, December 15, 1919, a fire that "...lighted up the sky for miles around and was easily visible from Bangor" swept through the buildings that comprised the Morris plant, and the B.N. Morris factory was at an end. High winds spread the fire quickly; firefighters from Veazie and Bangor worked to protect the nearby Congregational church and residential homes. The main office of the company, which contained the apartment of Bert Morris and his wife Margaret on its upper floor, suffered some fire-damage but was the only survivor. At the time of the fire, Margaret and Bert Morris were not at home; neither was Charlie Morris, who had driven himself and his daughter, Gladys, from their house on Flagg Street to Bangor in a carriage of Charlie's making, drawn by his horse Gypsy.

Reports of the fire found in Bangor's two newspapers dating from the following day and a report in an insurance company periodical, *The Standard*, dated December 20, 1919, are included in this chapter's Paddle Strokes. The *Bangor Daily News* reports that the fire began in the paint room and the *Daily Commercial* provides the Bangor fire chief's opinion that the fire began "above the boiler room" (which could have been the paint room, for all we now know). The December 20th issue of *The*

Standard states, "it is thought that the fire was caused by an overheated chimney." No subsequent reports exist in either of Bangor's two newspapers or the insurance companies' *Standard* to contradict this initial belief that the fire was accidental.

The earliest written material I have found stating arson was the cause of the Morris factory fire is the late Jean Hamilton's *History of Veazie*, published January 1, 1978. Ms. Hamilton states, "A fire caused by arson in 1920 destroyed Morris Canoe leaving about seventy five men unemployed. The business was never rebuilt. The arsonist was caught and punished." (It should be noted that the immediate post-fire story in *The Bangor Daily Commercial* states that 25 men were employed at the factory, not 75.)

Some accounts printed decades after the Morris factory's demise go into more detail than Ms. Hamilton's description, indicating the fire was started by an escapee from a mental institution, who set a number of fires in the Veazie area before being caught and incarcerated. Another version of the arson story involves a disgruntled former employee, seeking revenge for having been fired for drinking on the job.

While newspapers contemporary with the time of the fire fail to acknowledge the arson theory, the insurance company newspaper, *The Standard*, follows the adventures of a man named George B. Stanchfield, a ward of the State of Maine, while on parole from the Bangor Hospital for the Insane **five months after** the Morris fire. Stanchfield "went amok in Veazie", shooting a young woman with whom he was infatuated and setting fire to the barns of Austin Jones and Warren Prouty before being captured. The young lady survived, Stanchfield was interred in the

Augusta State Hospital, and Austin Jones was permitted to sue the State of Maine for damages-- receiving $23,650 in the end.

It would appear that The Public Mind incorporated the Morris fire into the tale of Mr. Stanchfield's rampage-- The Public Mind being more receptive to a colorful explanation of a disaster than to an explanation indicating accidental things could happen where unsprinklered wooden buildings containing wood, fiber, flammable liquids, machinery, furnaces fired by coal, and tall, creosote-filled chimneys exist.

It is reasonable to assume that Bert Morris insured the buildings largely because of fire-danger. The town of Veazie moved a hydrant to the State Street location in 1903, possibly at Bert's request, as he had enlarged the factory in 1902 and perhaps insurance premiums were less if there was a nearby water source for fire-fighters. A hydrant remains in that place to this day.

Losses due to the factory fire were estimated to reach $80,000, according to the insurance companies' *Standard* -- equivalent to $952,380 in 2014 dollars. Morris had the factory insured for $90,100, which is $1,073,000 in 2014 dollars.

The immediate post-fire newspaper accounts indicate the factory would be rebuilt. It appears this was still the plan when, on January 15, 1920, Bert Morris told a census enumerator that he was a "canvas canoe manufacturer" and Charles Morris stated he was a "machinist in a canoe shop".

In a special town meeting on January 7, 1920, the voters of Veazie agreed to exempt the B.N. Morris Company from local taxation for six years, provided the factory was rebuilt and operated as before the fire.

The Bangor papers describe a "large and enthusiastic attendance" that was concerned over the "many favorable offers [Morris had received] to relocate elsewhere". Old Town and Orono were among the suggested sites.

In the end, a rebuilt factory did not come to pass. Bert Morris explained that at 53, he was too old to begin again. Other factors may have played a part in this decision, and after a hard look at things, Bert decided to let the business go.

The simple inboard motor boat Morris offered in 1910 had not sold well due to the popularity of the outboard motor. While other major boat manufacturers continued to expand their lines, this level of competition may have been something Bert Morris did not wish to continue pursuing. His basic canoe hadn't undergone much change since he began building it in the early 1890s. By 1920, canoe builders were promoting the open gunwale for its practicality; Old Town would discontinue offering the closed gunwale by 1930. The Morris Outboard Motor Canoe and Morris Double Ended Boat, both offered for the first time in 1919, were built with open gunwales. Bert Morris may have been disinclined to abandon the use of his unique closed gunwale system on the canoe he'd built for decades; he was, after all, trained as a cabinet maker and had an eye for the way a canoe should appear.

However, Bert Morris was also a businessman. In 1916, the factory had again been expanded and the product-line tweaked to reflect a growing interest in canoes with long decks, torpedo-stems, and fancy painted designs. On February 6, 1918, the B.N. Morris Company was incorporated with capital stock of $100,000, of which $60,000 was common and $40,000 preferred. Bert is listed in *The Bangor Daily Commercial* as president and treasurer of the company and is one of its directors, along with three men from Bangor named Walter Brown, Harry Littlefield, and J. Herbert Boyd. Stock in the company never went public but was held by Bert and the three other company directors. The stated purpose of B.N. Morris, Inc., was "the manufacture and sale of canvas covered boats and canoes."

While competition with other boat builders continued to increase, financial upheavals following WWI caused fluctuations in canoe prices. Early in 1919, the Morris Company had been forced to raise the price of their wares by 25% due to a 10% governmental tax on sporting goods.

> ## 25% MUST BE ADDED TO ALL PRICES IN THIS CATALOGUE
>
> The government tax of 10% on canoes and fittings, together with the abnormal increase in cost of labor and materials compels us to advance our prices on everything listed in our catalogue twenty-five (25%) per-cent, until further notice.
>
> MORRIS CANOE COMPANY.

Image from 1919 catalog, courtesy *The Historic Wood Canoe and Boat Manufacturer Catalog Collection* edited by Daniel Miller and Benson Gray.

The manner in which the Morris Company was liquidated is unknown as well as whether Bert Morris was solvent or was left with a stack of bills even after insurance company payments.

In 1923, Bert Morris was approached by brothers Roland E. and

Forrest G. Lancaster of Bangor regarding a business opportunity. Born and raised in Veazie, the Lancasters operated a garage in Orono and had become agents for the Paige Detroit Motor Car Company. The brothers were interested in incorporating their business and expanding into adjacent counties. They may have required a monetary investment to make this plan work, and, having grown up in Veazie during the B.N. Morris Company's Golden Years, recognized the older man's history as head of a company that was among the first to sell a product via distributorships. The Morris name was placed first, and Bert was given the office of treasurer in the Morris-Lancaster Company—distributors of Paige and Jewett six cylinder automobiles, with sales and service offered at 50 Post Office Square in Bangor and dealerships in four Maine counties.

Advertisement in the Bangor City Directory

The Paige automobile is described as "the most beautiful car in America", reminiscent of advertisements for the High Grade B.N. Morris Canoe. In 1927, Paige Detroit was sold and the name of the car changed to Graham-Paige.

Paige advertisement in the *Saturday Evening Post* November 13, 1920

By 1927, Bert Morris is no longer listed as an officer of the Morris-Lancaster Company and may only have been involved initially. The 1930 census sees Bert Morris's name with a zero in the "occupation" category. The automobile dealership, which was among the largest in the Bangor area, continued to use the Morris name into the 1930s.

My mother used to spend a lot of time in the shop. Grampie Morris let her help build by sanding for him. She also spent time at the factory. She loved watching the men work. She said the canoes were beautiful. –Ellen Waltz, great-granddaughter of Charles Morris, recounting memories of her mother, Virginia King

Charlie Morris in 1927
(courtesy Ellen Waltz)

Following the factory fire, Charles Morris returned to building boats and canoes in the shop attached to the old Morris home in Veazie. His daughter, Gladys, had married a blacksmith named Bertram King in 1909, and they shared the Flagg Street house with Charlie. It was in this house that Gladys and Bert King's children, Virginia and Charles, were raised and learned some of the tricks of the boat-building trade when they helped Grampie Morris in his shop.

On the right is the ell that contained the carpentry shop attached to the Morris home in Veazie. The barn on the left can be accessed directly from both floors of the ell.

Charlie built his grandchildren each a sponson boat, described by great-grandson Louie King— son of Charles King—as being 19 feet long and canvas-covered. Young Charlie's boat had a transom for an outboard motor, but otherwise the boats built for Charles and Virginia were identical. As a child, Louie King used his father's boat on Pushaw Lake all summer for at least ten years, but he doesn't know what became of it.

The Pushaw Lake cottage had begun its life in the dooryard of the Veazie home, where Charles Morris pre-assembled it before hauling it twelve miles to lakeside for final assembly. The doors, windows, flooring and fancy gingerbread trim were made in the canoe shops. The cottage was equipped with kerosene lamps—some with reflectors and some with hand-painted globes. Great-grandson Louis King recalls that spaces between the studs in the cottage were lined with "a gold metallic paper of some sort" as a form of insulation. The cottage was sold in the late 1970s and moved to a lot on Pushaw Road. By then, it was already 90 years old.

The Morris cottage on Pushaw Lake in 1930. Ornate trim was created in the Morris canoe shops. (image courtesy Charlie's great-granddaughter, Ellen Waltz)

Louie King poses with Makela the pup on the dock at the family camp on Pushaw Lake, beside a rowboat built by his great-grandfather Charles Morris (courtesy Louie King)

Charles King with his son Louie at the family cottage on Pushaw Lake,
In front of a rowboat built by Charlie Morris (courtesy Louie King)

Louie King remembers boat building tools were kept in a shop on the upper floor of the ell attached to the family home on Flagg Street, and a sailboat built in that space was so large that the wall had to be opened to get the boat out. Ellen Waltz recalled her great-grandfather Charlie's shop as well. "I remember it as being full of tools, benches, canoe pieces and parts, and the smell of cedar. There were thwarts, ribs, etc. stored in barrels." Ellen recalled time spent fishing from the double ended rowboat Charlie had made for her mother—his granddaughter Virginia-- which was large enough for her parents and all four children in the family. Charlie Morris made things other than boats for his grandchildren. Virginia was given cross country skies, a toboggan, a cedar chest and a pine blanket chest. Virginia sold her boat to a man in Bucksport in 1963.

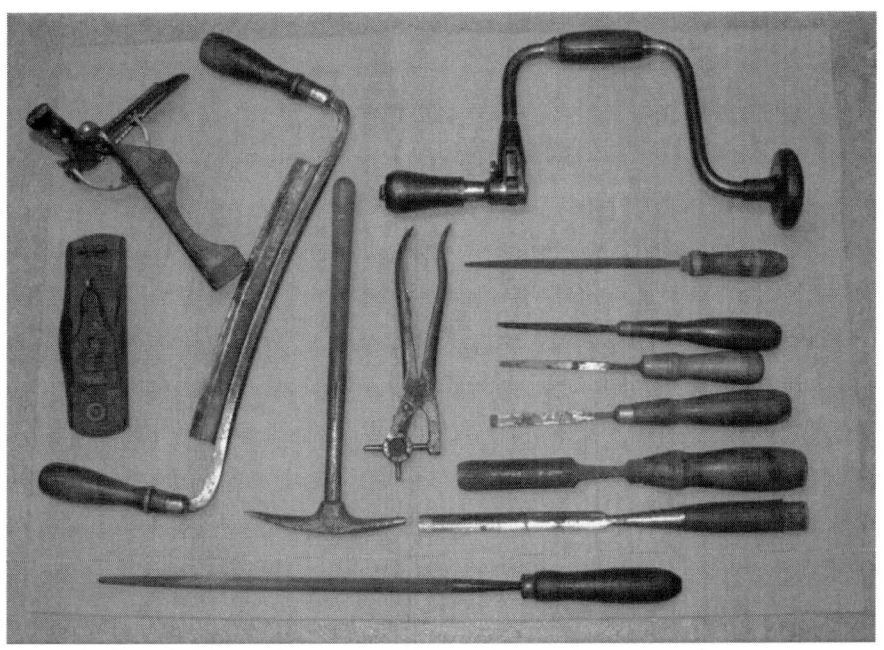

Tools once used by Charles Morris (courtesy Louie King)

In the Winter 1985 issue of *Wooden Canoe*, Charles King states his grandfather built all-wood racing canoes for Old Town following the demise of the Morris Company. There is anecdotal information that Bert Morris worked for Old Town following the factory fire, and circumstantial evidence suggests this may be true. The Old Town company took in canoes of any brand for repair; records of repairs are filed in the manner of the build records for Old Town boats. Among these repair records are thirteen Morris hulls that were completed at Old Town and shipped in 1921 and 1922. It is reasonable to assume that these canoes were finished under the supervision of Bert Morris.

Virginia King pictured in 1930 in bow of rowboat built for her by her grandfather, Charles Morris. With her is Helen Strickland, who would marry Virginia's brother, Charles King. (image courtesy Ellen Waltz)

More than one source has suggested that the Morris brothers built lapstrake canoes for Old Town. Lapstrake canoes are offered for the first time by Old Town on page 28 of the 1929 Old Town catalog. Charles Morris died on May 9, 1928; thus, Charlie didn't live long enough to be producing these particular boats for Old Town, but his younger brother— who had learned boat-building at his side-- may have done so. It should be remembered, however, that Charles A. Morris did more for canoe-building than teach and encourage his younger brother, Bert. As a machinist, Charlie helped mechanize the canoe building process, turning something done by a single individual into a situation where canoes were built by several men, each focused on a distinct part of the process.

The records of the Old Town Company contain information on lapstrake canoes that were numbered in a separate sequence. There are no construction-details on build records for these separately-sequenced boats, implying they might have been built outside the factory, on a subcontractual basis—possibly by Bert Morris. A January 1, 1930 Old Town factory inventory lists a 16 foot form for an all-cedar canoe with "Morris" in parentheses.

SHIPPED April 27- 1927
To Abercrombie & Fitch
New York City

Canoe No. 1
Our Order No.
Your Order No.

Via Special all Cedar Canoe
Length — Half Built
Grade — Model — Completed
Planking — Oiled
Gunwales — Canvassed
Decks — Filled
Thwarts — Stored
Seats — 2nd Filled
Half Ribs — Stored
Finish Rails — Railed
Keel — Fitted
O. S. Stems — Colored
Floor Rack — Varnished April 28-1927
Sponsons — Stored
Color Natural Wood

Courtesy Old Town Build Records on CD-ROM

Bert Morris

It is possible that Bert Morris was involved in canoe construction at the Kennebec factory in nearby Waterville after the fire. The relationship among the Maine canoe builders is not well-understood, but it would appear that an atmosphere of friendly competition existed. Certainly those at the Kennebec and Old Town companies could understand Bert Morris's tragic loss and find benefit in giving him a helping hand; Bert Morris was an experienced boat builder with many valuable contacts within the industry, and could have been regarded as a valuable resource. United States Census data gathered April 10, 1940, seven weeks prior to his death, lists Bert Morris's occupation as "boat builder" at a "boat factory", and he answered "yes" when questioned whether he worked for pay or profit. His obituary in the *Bangor Daily News* states, "... for the past four years he had been building in a portion of the factory of the Old Town Canoe Co."

··· FRIENDLY RIVALRY MAKES GOOD SPORT ···

In the spring of 1938, Minnesotan Joe Seliga wrote a letter to Bert Morris. Joe had grown up with two Morris canoes. He'd restored the family canoes and worked on those by other makers. Word of the Morris factory fire hadn't reached him, and he inquired about becoming a Morris agent. In his reply, Bert Morris explained that he was "not in the manufacturing business in a very big way", but was "building a few canoes every year". He offered Joe a discount and included a circular showing three models. Joe replied, suggesting they set up a protected distributorship. Bert Morris backed away from this offer, saying, "I am not building any great number of canoes, and do not wish to feel confined to building any particular number—I am doing this now-a-days more for a hobby" and offered to sell Joe an $85 canoe for $55. Joe Seliga decided instead to build his own canoes, based on the Morris; he would go on to become one of the foremost builders of wood and canvas canoes himself. Bell Canoe Works currently produces a model called the Seliga Tripper, based on Joe's canoe. Bert Morris may not have had any human children, but his life's work has produced many descendants.

Bert N. Morris died in his bed on May 31, 1940. His wife Margaret was in New York City at the time, visiting the World's Fair. With many years displaying boats at fairs far behind him, the old canoe builder stayed behind, preferring to spend his days in the shop and his evenings reading quietly at home. An account in the Bangor paper states that when Bert was found, "the light by which he had been reading was still burning."

Giving Bert a friendly pat at Mount Hope Cemetery in Bangor

Morris family at Mount Hope: Bert, Gracie, Charlie, Sophronia, and Albion;
Charlie's daughter Gladys and her husband rest on the other side of the family monument

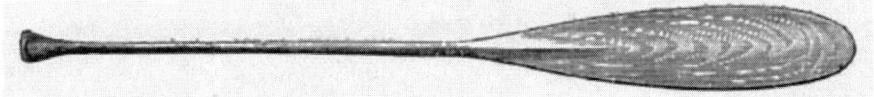

Paddle Strokes 10
Tracking the Journey...

From the *Bangor Daily Commercial*, December 16, 1919:

MORRIS CANOE PLANT AT VEAZIE DESTROYED

Heavy Loss Results From Fire Monday Evening; Will Be Rebuilt

Fire which completely destroyed the buildings of the Morris Canoe Company's plant in Veazie Monday evening caused a loss which has been approximated at over $50,000 and put out of commission temporarily one of the busiest and most active industries in this section of the state.

The fire, which in the opinion of Chief Mason started above the boiler room, was discovered about 5:30 o'clock, and had spread rapidly before any assistance could be reached. The Bangor department was notified and Chief Mason and the auto truck with a crew of men responded. When the Bangor apparatus reached there the fire had got well under way, it having spread quickly, and it was clearly evident that the important job was to save the surrounding buildings.

A large part of the building in which the office was located was saved as was another dwelling house only a few feet away by the line of hose laid by the Bangor firemen. In five minutes' time the loss was terrific and there was a high wind to fan the fire. The fire lighted up the sky for miles around and was easily visible from Bangor.

The principal loss was in the buildings, with the heavy stock a close second. There was approximately $10,000 worth of canvas on hand at the plant with a large amount of lumber, brass, copper and other articles, used in the manufacture of canoes, in addition to a large number of finished canoes. An official of the company stated Tuesday morning that nearly all the canoes that were on hand were a total loss.

The plant was heavily insured and several policies were carried by Bangor companies, among whom were listed the following: L.C. Tyler & Sons agency, $8,500; W.W. Palmer, $5,000; and Pearl & Dennett, $10,400. In addition to this there is about $60,000 carried by the Massachusetts Mutual Co.

The Morris plant was well equipped and has been doing a big business. The plant will be rebuilt as soon as possible, according to an announcement made Monday morning from the office of the company. This plant was started about 30 years ago and B.N. Morris has been continually adding to it until it has reached its present standing among the industries of the state.

From the *Bangor Daily News*, December 16, 1919:

MORRIS CANOE PLANT WIPED OUT

Was a Prosperous Industry at Veazie-- Loss Estimated at $75,000

Fire which broke out about 5:30 o'clock Monday night spread with great rapidity through the group of half a dozen wooden buildings making up the B.N. Morris canoe plant at Veazie and all were wiped out with the exception of the office building, also occupied by B.N. Morris as living apartments which was partially burned. The plant was in full operation employing about 25 hands. Nearly all the finished canoes on hand were saved but much expensive material including $50,000 worth of canvas, a large amount of various kinds of lumber and other stock was lost. Mr. Morris was unable to give an estimate of his total loss last night, but it will be not far from $75,000. Bangor agencies carried insurance of $23,000 distributed, $8500 on the L.C. Tyler & Sons agency, $5000 with W.W. Palmer and $10,400 with Pearl & Dennett. It is understood that there was other insurance in mutual companies.

The fire was very spectacular, lighting up the country for miles around. Help was called from Bangor and Chief Mason and the motor truck went up. At one time the situation looked serious with brands and sparks showering the residences adjoining and the Congregational church but with the hydrant service and hard fighting by the Veazie and Bangor firemen the damage was held to the Morris plant. The office building was saved although the apartments of Mr. Morris were partly burned and his furniture got out in a somewhat damaged condition. The cause of the fire appears to be uncertain, breaking out in the paint shops.

The Morris plant was well equipped and doing a good business, turning out a product in good demand all over the country and being a much appreciated industry for the town. It is understood that the plant will be rebuilt at once.

From *The Standard*, December 20, 1919:

CANOE FACTORY HAS HEAVY LOSS

Veazie, Me., December 15—Fire early today caused a heavy loss at the plant of the B.N. Morris Canoe Factory. The total damage may reach $80,000. All of the buildings and contents with the exception of the office building and a few canoes were totally destroyed. The buildings were of frame and unsprinklered. It is thought that the fire was caused by an overheated chimney.

Indiana Lumbermen's Mu.	$5,500	Penn. Millers' Mutual	$3,000
Lumbermen's Mu., Ohio	5,500	New Hampshire	3,000
Penn. Lumber Mutual	5,500	Grain Dealers Mutual	2,750
Lumber Mutual, Boston	5,500	Minn. Impl. Mutual	2,500
Central Mfgrs. Mutual	5,500	American Central	2,500
National	5,300	Home	2,500
Millers' Mutual	5,000	Springfield, F. & M.	2,500
Northwestern Mutual	4,750	Ohio Mutual	2,000
Phil. Und.	4,000	Mansfield Mutual	2,000
Grain Dealers' Mutual	4,000	Niagara	1,500
Meschts. & Mfrs. Mutuals		Sun	1,300
Mansfield	4,000	Automobile	1,000
Mill Owners	4,000		
Fitchburg Mutual	3,000	Total	$90,100

List posted in *The Standard* showing Morris held policies totaling $90,100.00

From *The Old Town Enterprise,* April 3, 1920:

We have two canoe plants, why not have three? Morris canoe plant in Veazie was burned to the ground several months ago, and he will probably not rebuild there. It has been suggested to him that he come to Old Town there centralizing the canoe business in this vicinity at least. We understand he thought there might be something in the area and perhaps might consider it before starting out again. We understand he employed

25 to 30 hands. While the proposition has not taken any definite form perhaps by exercising a little interest and activity by some of the citizens or organizations, we might be able to get another industry. One of our well known citizens has conferred with Mr. Morris on the subject.

From *The Old Town Enterprise*, Orono News Section, March 9, 1912:

It is too bad Morris canoe in Veazie could not be moved to this town and placed beside the Shaw & Tenney factory near the railroad where it could have better railroad facilities and boom Orono. We have no evil designs on Veazie but wish them well.

Photo found in the former Morris home In Veazie may be that of an elderly Bert Morris

Many thanks to the descendants of Charles Morris who shared pictures and family stories. I am saddened knowing I won't be thanking Charlie's great-granddaughter Ellen Waltz in-person, as she passed away in August of 2013. Her enthusiasm for this project has been greatly appreciated and is sorely missed.

Additional Resources:

Stelmok, Jerry, *The Art of the Canoe with Joe Seliga*, MBI Publishing Company, 2002.

A tribute to Joe Seliga, *See you 'Round the Bend*, can be found at: http://www.youtube.com/watch?v=c26qwzutxec (Words and music by Pat Surface)

Joe Seliga inspects Morris 11857 (courtesy Curt Carlson)

Maine Liable for Maniac Act

A decision of the Maine law court of far-reaching importance, in that it establishes the liabilty of the state in certain cases, has been rendered in the civil acton, authorized by the Maine legislature, of the Austin W. Jones Company of Bangor and Veazie against the state of Maine to recover damages for the loss of farm buildings and stock which were destroyed by fire by a lunatic released on parole from the Bangor State Hospital.

The law court sustains the verdict of the jury of $23,650 damages, deducting, however, $500 held to be only speculative damage for loss of the prospective value of young stock, held not to be recoverable. Interest from the date of the writ is allowed.

On a stormy Saturday night in May, 1920, George B. Stanchfield of Veazie, who had been released on parole from the Bangor State Hospital following his escape from that institution by swimming the river and his return to the hospital by his mother, ran amuck in Veazie. He went to the home of the young woman to whom he believed himself in love and fired a gun through the window into the room in which the girl and her mother were asleep. Fortunately the girl was not fatally injured.

The maniac then went to the Jones Company farm and the Prouty place near by, setting fire to their barns, destroying them and much of the contents, including some blooded stock at the Jones place.

Stanchfield was arrested after an exciting chase. He escaped from the officers by a ruse, but was recaptured very soon. He was sent from the superior court in Bangor to the department for criminal insane at the Augusta State Hospital.

In March, 1921, the legislature passed a resolve awarding damages to the Jones Company, but this was vetoed by the governor, and later a resolve was passed by the legislature authorizing the Austin W. Jones Company to bring suit against the state.

The case was heard at the November term of the superior court in 1921, and the jury awarded plaintiffs damages in the sum of $23,650. The attorney-general took the case to the law court.

The colorful story of a "lunatic run amok" is a likely basis for some stories regarding the Morris factory fire. This follow-up account appears in the insurance companies' February 17, 1923 issue of *The Standard*. (document found at Harvard University Library and acquired through inter-library loan by Howard Herman-Haase)

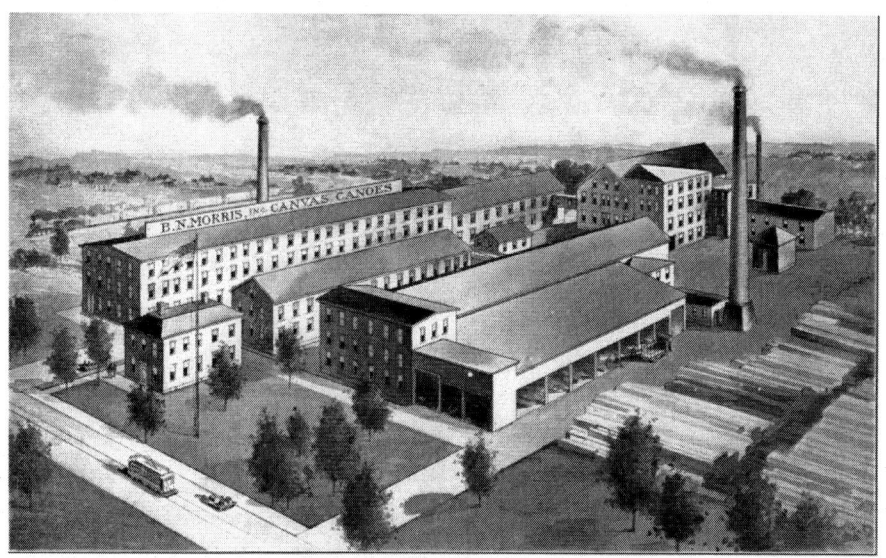

FACTORIES OF B. N. MORRIS, INC., VEAZIE, MAINE
BUILDERS OF THE MORRIS CANOE

Morris factory as pictured in the 1917 catalog. The building that survived the fire is the structure closest to the road.

Former B. N. Morris office and residence as it appeared in 2014

11

UP FROM THE ASHES

The question is often asked, "What is the life of a canvas canoe?" The experience of years of use and familiarity with this type indicates that its usefulness is terminated by accident or abuse, never by old age.
--Bert N. Morris

World War II followed upon the heels of Bert Morris's death, and the post-war period saw an economic boom offering new products and services that left some things considered "old fashioned" behind. Boats of wood and canvas gave way to those of aluminum and fiberglass and the name "Old Town" was applied to wooden canoes in general. It was with the formation of the Wooden Canoe Heritage Association in 1979 that the Morris canoe was rediscovered.

When wooden canoe enthusiasts assembled to compare what they were paddling, canoes of the B.N. Morris Company stood out. Jill and Jeff Dean—who are among the initial founders of the Wooden Canoe Heritage Association-- took an especial interest in Morris after restoring two Morris canoes that have since been donated to the Wisconsin Canoe Heritage Museum. The Winter 1985 issue of *Wooden Canoe* contains a summary by the Deans of what was then known about the Morris canoe and the company that built it. They describe the attention paid Morrises that were present at the 1984 WCHA Assembly in Dorset, Ontario, where

"Morris canoes were among the most highly regarded and praised. Those who have seen a well restored or preserved Morris understand why this is so. Most striking are the grace and esthetics of the lines of the Morris. Then follow the precision and quality of the woodwork and details of construction. Though there are other canoes that are better suited for certain purposes, some would argue that Morris built the best wood-and-canvas canoes ever made; most would agree that they rank up there with the best."

The Deans' Model B type 2 Morris, now in the collection of the Wisconsin Canoe Heritage Museum. Image appears on the cover of the Winter 1985 *Wooden Canoe* and in the Wikipedia article on the B.N. Morris Canoe Company. (photo by Jeff Dean)

The resurrection of the Morris was assisted by the fact that their unusual stems made them easy to identify, and although they didn't exist in great numbers, those who wanted one could find one. For anyone interested in paddling a historic canoe, the Morris became a prize worth seeking.

Tom MacKenzie and Clyde Gallup examine a Morris at the 1984 WCHA Assembly in Ontario (*Wooden Canoe* 21, Winter 1985, p.6)

It was soon learned that the Morris name hadn't been completely forgotten in the decades between 1920 and 1980. WCHA member and canoe builder Joe Seliga shared stories of his family's Morrises, his contact with Bert, and his decision to build canoes based on the Morris. In an article in the spring 1984 issue of *Wooden Canoe,* Joe extolled the attributes of the canoe that had made a profound impression on his life.

"I don't think anybody built a finer canoe than B.N. Morris," he states in the article. "It's a canoe that when it gets in the water... it's like a swan. Proud."

Some canoes built by Morris contemporaries show a Morris-influence. The Chestnut Company of New Brunswick modeled its early canoes on the Morris, but without a splayed cedar stem and pocketed ribs. Rushton's first-grade Indian Girl model has pocketed ribs. Rhinelander Canoe and Boat states in their catalogs that their canoes are based on "the Morris pattern", some appearing to be Morris in every way, except the splayed stem is ash and the seats in later canoes are not hand-caned. Modern professional shops such as Northwoods Canoe in Maine, McCurdy and Reed in Nova Scotia, and Ambrose Canoe in Alabama offer Morris reproductions, and plans exist for the hobby builder to use.

The first official WCHA tee shirt, designed by Jerry Stelmok in 1982, features the Morris Special Indian image that would become part of the group's logo. (*Wooden Canoe* 12, Autumn 1982, p.2)

Morris was the featured canoe of the 1997 Assembly of the Wooden Canoe Heritage Association at Paul Smith's College of the Adirondacks. A tee shirt made for this occasion features the cover-image of Morris's 1917 catalog on the back. Morris is the featured canoe of the 2015 Assembly, when more Morris canoes may be assembled in one place than at any time since the factory's end.

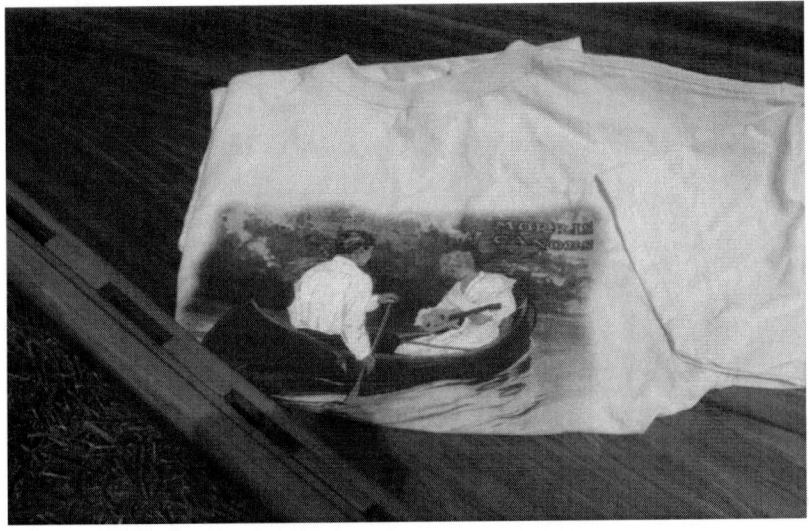

Tee shirt designed for the 1997 WCHA Assembly (image from listing in the WCHA on-line Store, where this item is currently offered for sale)

As with any wood-canvas canoe, the B.N. Morris can be brought from the brink of the burn-pile to float upon water again, because it is made of component parts, each of which can be replaced if damaged. It is my hope that images and discussion contained in this book are helpful in making old Morris canoes appear as once they did. The following resources for restoration of any wood and canvas canoe are available through the WCHA Store, and some are available wherever books are found:

Stelmok, Jerry and Rollin Thurlow, *The Wood & Canvas Canoe: A Complete Guide to Its History, Construction, Restoration, and Maintenance*, The Harpswell Press, 1987.

Stelmok, Jerry, *Building the Maine Guide Canoe*, International Marine Publishing Company, 1980.

Stelmok, Jerry, *The Art of the Canoe with Joe Seliga*, MBI Publishing Company, 2002.

Rebuilding the Wood & Canvas Canoe: Reprints of three articles from *Wooden Canoe Journal* and *Wooden Boat* magazine, available through the WCHA Store.

Simmons, Walter J., *Repairs* and *Finishing*, both available through the WCHA Store.

There are many who restore boats for a living, if one does not wish to tackle the job themselves. This is personally where I stand: I can work with paint stripper, do a bit of sanding, apply varnish, and cane a seat... but I preferred to turn my sweet old canoe over to a woodworker for the job of repairing her broken and missing bits. It may seem I am on a WCHA Bandwagon because I am about to encourage anyone interested in wooden canoes to look over the website and pop into the Forums, but here's the thing: there simply isn't a better group of people around. So, hop on the bandwagon with me-- even if you don't have a wooden canoe... yet (an appreciation of them can be rather contagious).

The Forums on the website of the Wooden Canoe Heritage Association (www.wcha.org) offer an opportunity to post specific questions, to share the details of a restoration, or to simply show off what you have.

B.N. Morris 1703, mid-restoration (courtesy Dave Houston)

Morris Stain Recipe

The spruce gunwales and cedar interiors of many Morris canoes were originally stained to match their mahogany parts. The stain color has been referred to as "pigeon blood", but Denis Kallery worked out a recipe without harming any pigeons. Using Minwax products, by unit (meaning eye-dropper-full, teaspoon, cup, truckload, what-have-you):

2 parts Red Mahogany #225
2 parts Golden Oak #210B
1 part Special Walnut #224
1 part Sedona Red #222

Denis Kallery stripping the interior of Morris 15768, a Belle Isle canoe

Canoes on the green: WCHA Assembly 2014, Paul Smith's College of the Adirondacks
(courtesy Fred Campbell)

12

DATING A MORRIS CANOE

*You don't need to take her to dinner—
even a courting canoe has no such expectation!*

"Who made my canoe?" may be the first question the owner of an old wood-canvas asks, followed by "How old is it?" Unfortunately, the records of the Morris Company haven't been found; they may have been lost in the factory fire or destroyed when it seemed the business would not be rebuilt—or Morris may not have kept records. With renewed interest in the Morris following the formation of the Wooden Canoe Heritage Association, theories based on the canoe's serial numbering emerged and have been refined over time. Discussion of the progression of thought that led to the current Morris-dating-theory is included in this chapter's Paddle Strokes.

Morris Canoe with Serial Number

The stem on the floor of the canoe is a common place to find a canoe's serial number, if there is one. Old Town serial numbers are found tamped directly into the wood on both stems; they consist of five or six numbers followed by a space and then the length of the canoe. Records exist that connect the serial number on an Old Town boat or canoe to details of its construction (the "build record"), including the date it was shipped—its "birthday".

B.N. Morris placed serial numbers on a brass plate, attached either to the stem at the bow end or on the left inwale, near the bow end. Morris serial numbers consist of five or fewer digits. There is no "code" built into a Morris serial number; that is, canoe number 7630 was simply the 7,630th B.N. Morris canoe built since numbering began. For some companies, numbering canoes was a means by which they kept track of inventory, and records of the building process a means of keeping track of who did the work.

Serial number ranges offered in the table in this chapter are based on seven known shipping-dates, the serial numbers of Morris hulls that were completed at Old Town Canoe, and records of the Old Town Canoe Company that suggest highs and lows in canoe sales over the course of Morris's production years.

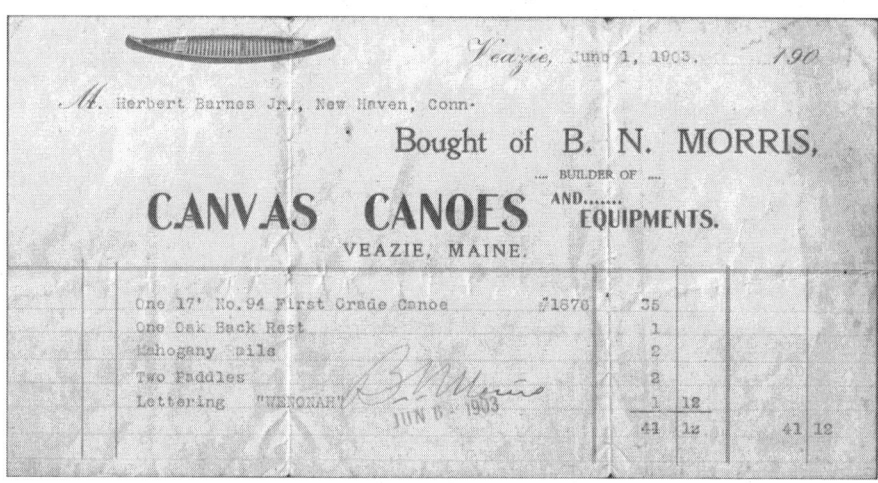

Receipt for Morris #1876, dated June 1, 1903, was offered on eBay

The table on the next page suggests Morris #7630 was completed in 1911. Because it is the first number listed in the 1911 category, it could easily have been completed in 1910. Using the word "circa" when talking about the date of a specific Morris canoe comes in handy, as it means "around the time of". The date might be off by a year or so, but old ladies sometimes prefer not to provide their exact age.

Morris Date and Serial Number Table

Date	Serial Number
1900	1-469
1901	470-985
1902	986-1556
1903	1557-2182
1904	2183-2873
1905	2874-3574
1906	3575-4325
1907	4326-5101
1908	5102-5902
1909	5903-6753
1910	6754-7629
1911	7630-8567
1912	8568-9543
1913	9544-10694
1914	10695-12045
1915	12046-13546
1916	13547-14897
1917	14898-15798
1918	15799-16499
1919	16500-17263

(courtesy Michael Cyr)

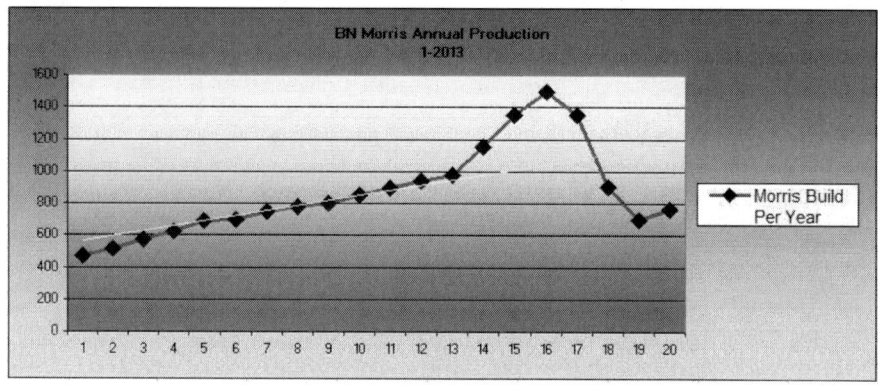

Morris Annual Production (courtesy Michael Cyr)

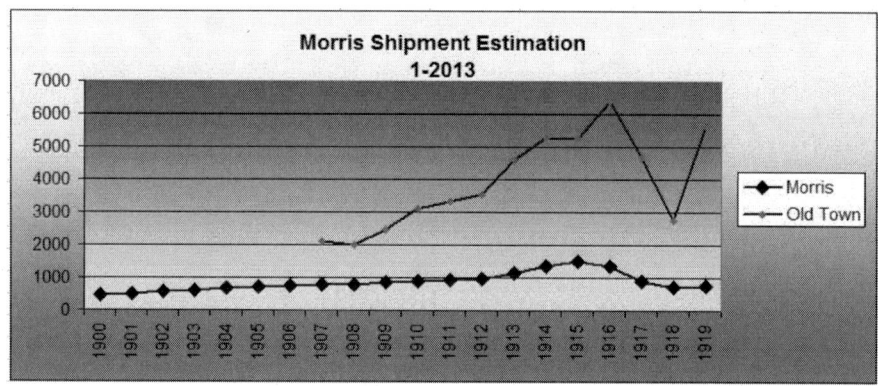

Morris Shipment Estimation (courtesy Michael Cyr)

With B.N. Morris canoes, serial numbers consisting of four digits will be found on a 1 ½ inches by 5/8 inch oval brass plate affixed with two escutcheon pins to the left inwale just beyond the bow deck—often directly over the first full rib. A serial number five digits long will be found on a 1½ inches by ½ inch rectangular plate with rounded corners, attached to the bow stem with four escutcheon pins. A canoe with a four-digit serial number on a rectangular plate on the stem is a Veazie Canoe Company canoe (discussed in Chapter 9) unless there is an initial "hidden

1"; when a rectangular plate on the stem appears to consist of only four numbers, it pays to carefully scrutinize the area between the two escutcheon pins on the left for a "1".

This poorly-centered serial number appeared to be "3724" prior to cleaning it up. Screws affixing it to the stem are not original to the canoe but replaced the escutcheon pins.

In the latter years of Morris production, the rectangular serial number plate was occasionally placed on a seat-frame if the canoe had long decks.

Rectangular serial number plate on seat frame of Greg Briggs' Morris
(courtesy John Naylor)

Oval serial number plate on left inwale

Morris Canoe without Serial Number

There are a few things to look for when a Morris canoe doesn't have a brass serial number plate on the stem or inwale. If the canoe has long decks, the plate may be on one of the seat frames. In building a Morris, the brass plate was one of the last things attached to the canoe and rather than crawling under a long deck to pound a tack hammer (especially on a Friday night), it apparently seemed preferable in a few cases to tack the tag to the frame of the bow seat.

If no plate can be found, there may be tell-tale tack-holes. The inwale-location is above or near the first full rib on the left side. Holes are about 1 5/16 inches apart. If holes are there, the canoe was probably built after 1900 but before 1910, when the rectangular plate came into use. This date can be further honed by counting the number of **cant rib** pairs. Cant ribs are located in the bow and stern. They aren't full, steam-bent ribs, but are partial ribs that are canted into the stem to provide strength to the ends of the canoe. Morris canoes were built with two pairs of cant ribs until about 1905, when a third set was introduced high into the nose without changing the shape of the canoe. Therefore, if a Morris canoe has two tack holes in the inwale and two pairs of cant ribs, it can be said it was built between 1900 and 1905; if it has three pairs of cant ribs and two inwale tack holes, it likely dates from 1905-1910.

Tack holes in inwale of Morris

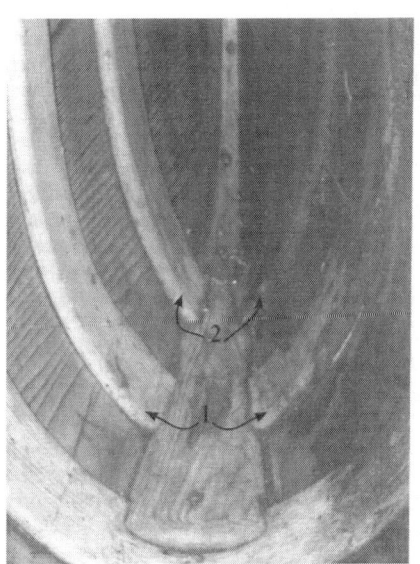 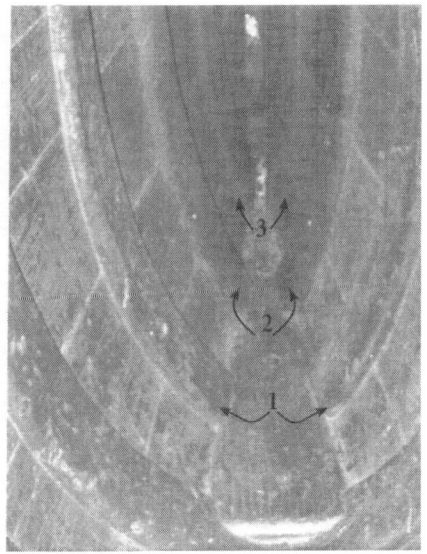

Morris with two pairs of cant ribs on left and three pairs on right

The bow stem position for the serial number plate involves four tack holes, 1 ¼ inches apart on the longer side and 7/16 inch apart on the shorter. If there are signs of tack holes on the stem, the canoe is circa 1910-1920. Additional factors may hone the dates a bit. The rectangular plate is usually oriented with the long side parallel to the end of the stem and the ribs, but in the years 1912-1916 a number of canoes have a plate rotated ninety degrees, so that the short side is parallel to the splay of the stem. It seems a factory worker may have marked the canoes he worked on in this manner; therefore, even without a serial number plate, "rotated holes" places a canoe in the 1912-16 range, described as "SN Plate or tack holes Located on Stem (Perpendicular to Ribs)" in the table on page 189. A canoe with Special Ends ("torpedo" stems as described on page 76 and pictured on page 102) suggest a Model A built between 1916-1920.

The Wehling family's Morris has a serial number plate in the "rotated" position.
(photo courtesy Dave Osborn)

If there is no sign of a serial number plate having been tacked to the stem, the inwale, or a seat frame AND the canoe has only two pairs of cant ribs, the canoe was likely built before 1900. Those canoes with a metal nameplate stating "From The Morris Canoe Factory" (p. 69) pre-date the use of the decal and are possibly circa 1894-1897. The metal

"Builder" tag (p. 63) suggests a pre-1894 canoe. Canoes with two pairs of cant ribs and no sign of a serial number plate or Morris nameplate may be circa 1897-1900.

Information available in *The Historic Wooden Boat and Canoe Manufacturer Catalog Collection* has been a great help identifying and dating other Morris printed matter and Morris equipment. Decal-type, discussed on page 104, may also help date a canoe.

Guide for Dating Morris Canoes

Morris SN	Year	No Morris SN Available			Year
Not Applicable	1890	No SN Plate or Tack Holes	Tack Holes on Thwarts	"Builder" Tag on Thwart	1890
	1891				1891
	1892				1892
	1893				1893
	1894			"Factory" Tag on Thwart	1894
	1895				1895
	1896				1896
	1897				1897
	1898		No Tag or Tack Holes on Thwarts		1898
	1899				1899
1 - 469	1900	SN Plate or Tack Holes on Inwale	Two Pairs of Cant Ribs		1900
470 - 985	1901				1901
986 - 1556	1902				1902
1557 – 2182	1903				1903
2183 - 2873	1904				1904
2874 - 3574	1905		Three Pairs of Cant Ribs		1905
3575 - 4325	1906				1906
4326 - 5101	1907				1907
5102 - 5902	1908				1908
5903 - 6753	1909				1909
6754 - 7629	1910	SN Plate or Tack Holes on Stem (Perpendicular to Ribs)	SN Plate or Tack Holes on Stem (Parallel to Ribs)		1910
7630 - 8567	1911				1911
8568 - 9543	1912				1912
9544 - 10694	1913				1913
10695 - 12045	1914				1915
12046 - 13546	1915				1915
13547 - 14897	1916			Torpedo Ends	1916
14898 - 15798	1917				1917
15799 - 16499	1918				1918
16500 - 17263	1919				1919

(Table courtesy Howard Herman-Haase)

The table on page 189 consolidates the table on page 183 with factors that may help place a date on Morris canoes without a serial number. Dotted horizontal lines indicate dates that are more speculative than solid horizontal lines. It should be noted that canoes were shipped from the factory in order of their completion, so a canoe with a higher serial number may have shipped prior to one with a lower number; again, using "circa" keeps us honest!

Ken and Mary Kelly enjoy quiet waters and Morris 16214

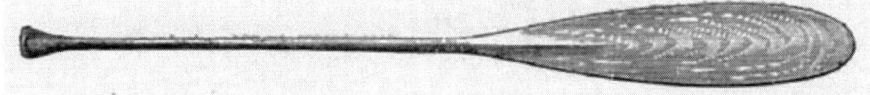

Paddle Strokes 12

Tracking the Journey...

With the re-discovery of the Morris canoe in the late 1970s came an interest in determining if there was any significance to the numbers found on the brass plates that were attached either to the stem or inwale. The current system for dating Morris canoes evolved over time, as information sifted into the awareness of those concerned with placing a specific date on each canoe. The following is a discussion of the progression of thought behind the numbers found on Morris canoes.

Initial Theories

Jill and Jeff Dean, who were among the initial founders of the Wooden Canoe Heritage Association, took an especial interest in the Morris canoe. The dating of these canoes is initially discussed by the Deans in issue 21 of *Wooden Canoe*, Winter 1985. The previous winter, WCHA member Morrison Brinker suggested to them that Morris canoes might be dated using their serial numbers. The Deans followed up on this suggestion, and after surveying the serial numbers of 23 Morris canoes belonging to WCHA members, agreed that the serial numbers on Morris canoes suggested a date. Under the Brinker Theory, the first two digits of a five-digit serial number equaled the last two digits of the canoe's year of production. Under this theory, Morris 13547 was built in 1913.

Nine canoes with four-digit serial numbers turned up in the course of the Deans' survey, and the Brinker Theory was refined to include the suggestion that with four-digit serial numbers, the first digit suggested the year of the canoe's completion. Under this revised theory—initially referred to as The Brinker-Dean Theory-- canoe 9762 would have been built in 1909 and canoe 13547 in 1913. As with the current theory of Morris-dating, Brinker-Dean supposed that Morris began using serial numbers in 1900; however, the theory implies that Morris deliberately built the year of production into their serial numbers, and it was further suggested that the remaining numbers in a serial number might indicate how many canoes had been produced so-far that year. Therefore, under Brinker-Dean, canoe 9762 might have been the 762nd canoe built by Morris in 1909. It is now understood that the numbers are purely sequential with no built-in coding.

A Dating Formula

Following the Winter of 1985 call for a collection of serial numbers, the Deans proposed a formula which might be used to obtain a more accurate date for a Morris canoe, as it seemed Morris might not have begun re-numbering canoes on January first of each year. They suggested dividing the serial number by 750 and then adding 1900 (Year=serial number/750 + 1900). Using this formula, canoe 9762 went from being a 1909 canoe to a 1911 canoe, and 13547 went from 1913 to 1918. This theory assumes the quantity of canoes produced remained constant from year to year. It works well for lower serial numbers -- Morris 9456, which records show was shipped April 9, 1912, comes out

"1912" after the math is done; but when the formula is applied to the larger five-digit serial numbers, results may be several years off-- some dating after the factory's demise. The formula didn't catch on well, although memories of it were still around when I got my first Morris and was told not to simply use the first two digits to find the shipping date-- I should divide it by "some number" (long forgotten) to accurately know when it had been born.

Brinker-Dean, Plus Two

The Brinker-Dean Theory, proven to be easiest for Morris owners to use, was honed in 1996 following a serendipitous find. While investigating the possibility of scanning build records of the Old Town Canoe Company, Tim Hewitt and Benson Gray found documentation of thirteen Morris hulls that were completed at Old Town within their repair records. It appeared the hulls had been numbered by Morris, and none was higher than 17263. It was then suggested that adding "two" to the number or numbers found using the Brinker-Dean Theory could provide a fairly accurate date, as Morris hull 17263 was obviously built in 1919.

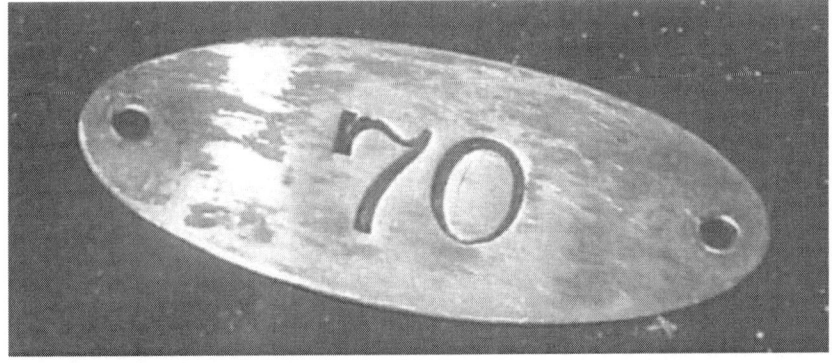

Lowest serial number of a B.N. Morris canoe in the Morris Database (courtesy Ian Conk)

In the early 1980s, the lowest Morris number known was four digits long, and any canoes without a number were thought to have lost their tag. With only a handful of canoes upon which to base any theories, the shape and placement of the serial number plate was not discussed, and there was no observed pattern to the changes in the canoes themselves upon which to place a date, other than the fact that later Morrises appeared to have more recurve, or "torpedo", in their profile. The Brinker-Dean, Plus Two Theory stood as the best suggestion of Morris canoe age until further discoveries permitted a table to be developed.

SHIPPED June 28 1921 B. N. Morris		Canoe No. 17263
To Milton E Norman		Our Order No. 3723
4928 Kenmore Ave		Your Order No.
Chicago, Ill.		
Via		
Length 18		Half Built
Grade 3	Model a	Completed
Planking closed mahog		Oiled
Gunwales spruce		Canvassed
Decks 36" Birch 24" stern		Filled
Thwarts middle		Stored
Seats		2nd Filled
Half Ribs		Stored
Finish Rails		Railed
Keel yes		Fitted
O. S. Stems yes		Colored
Floor Rack yes		Varnished
Sponsons		Stored
Color		

1-20-10,000

Record of a Morris hull that was finished at Old Town and shipped in 1921. With 36" bow decks and 24 inch stern decks, it was a Morris Molitor. This canoe has yet to appear in the database. (from the Old Town Build Records on CD-ROM)

Date and Serial Number Table

In 2007, a call for information on existing Morris-built canoes and boats was put out resulting in creation of a database of more than 300. The database has provided examination of discrete differences in Morris canoes over time, which has helped to establish the age of those without a serial number and to firm-up a theory that provides a more exact year for those canoes where a number exists. The eleven Morris catalogs have been carefully scrutinized to fit with what the existing canoes tell us. On-line availability of scanned documents has yielded information that helps tell the Morris story, and the occasional bills, receipts and business-letters that have surfaced in recent years have been particularly exciting finds.

Ephemera is defined in the Wikipedia as "any transitory written or printed matter not meant to be retained or preserved. The word derives from the Greek, meaning things lasting no more than a day." The current dating theory regarding Morris canoes relies on bits of paper that might have been thrown away, but were not. These bits include the receipt for Morris 1878, which was found on eBay, receipt for Morris 9023 submitted with the canoe when it was donated to the museum in Mystic Seaport, and information on five canoes found within a stack of 1911-1912 Morris receipts by the current owner of the Morris home in Veazie and donated to our research.

There have also been letters addressed to Bert Morris dating from the 1890s which help in understanding the canoe models produced then and shed light on the way business was conducted. WCHA member and Morris reproduction builder Rollin Thurlow received a group of nine such letters, and Paul Miller found a group offered on eBay. As time goes on, perhaps more such "magical finds" will occur, and the Morris Dating System will be honed again.

When WCHA member Michael Cyr initially took on the task of creating a table correlating Morris serial numbers with possible shipping-dates, receipts for canoe 1878, shipped June 6, 1903, and canoe 9023, shipped May 15, 1912, were the only exact ship-dates we had to go on. The information provided by the five additional serial numbers found in the 1911-1912 Morris receipts appears to confirm that we are on the right-track with our current Morris-dating-scheme: these additional serial numbers didn't shift the numbers in the table.

An invoice involving the Morris dealership in Minneapolis shows that canoes numbered 8435 and 8308 were shipped April 27, 1911. They are described as being Model A, Type 1, original color light C.P. Green. Morris canoes 7974 and 7969, also Model A (no color mentioned) were shipped April 28, 1911; 7974 was returned to the factory May 16th. Also found was the receipt for canoe 9456, which apparently arrived at the dealership in Grand Rapids, Michigan, in need of touching-up by a local craftsman, for which the Morris Company was billed ten dollars on April 19, 1912.

This serial-number find gave me a chill like the touch of a hand on my shoulder, as one of the four canoes shipped to Minneapolis in 1911 was a canoe Denis Kallery and I owned. Morris number 8435 was the canoe I used in a YouTube video to demonstrate the features of a B.N. Morris canoe. I like the serendipity of that.

I must again thank all who provided information to the Morris database, Michael Cyr for putting the date-table together, Howard

Herman-Haase for creating the guide that includes canoes without a serial number, Benson Gray for information on Old Town's output in specific years, and Jill and Jeff Dean and the late Dave Baker for their initial work in bringing the Morris to light.

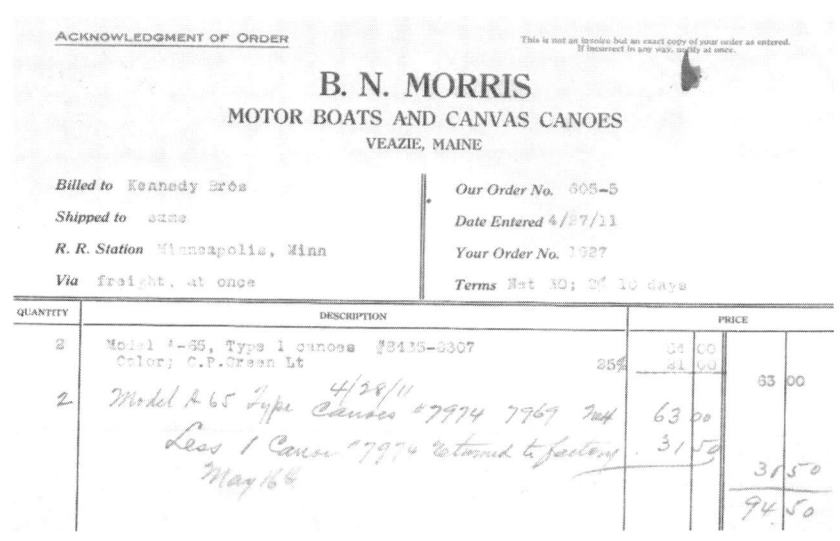

Morris invoice for canoes shipped to Kennedy Bros. in Minneapolis in 1911

Denis Kallery loads Morris 8435, originally shipped to Kennedy Bros. in 1911

| C. B. KELSEY, Pres. | JAMES BAYNE, Vice Pres. | W. B. JARVIS, Sec.-Treas. |

W. B. JARVIS CO.
WHOLESALE AND RETAIL
SPORTSMEN'S SUPPLIES, BICYCLES, SUNDRIES, ATHLETIC GOODS
GUNS, AMMUNITION AND CUTLERY
204 MONROE AVENUE

ORDER NO. 5003 D   DATE Apr. 19, 1912   GRAND RAPIDS, MICH.

SOLD TO B.N. Morris, Veazie, Me.

TERMS	SHIPPED VIA		
To refinishing #9456 Canoe			10.00

Invoice sent to Morris Company to cover cost of repair to canoe that arrived damaged

Kathy Klos and Denis Kallery paddle Veazie canoe 1032 with pups Charlie and Bert in the paddle-by at a WCHA Assembly in Peterborough, Ontario; the canoe is likely c.1915-16 based on a "rotated" serial number plate and the fact that Veazie 716 is c.1913.
(photo courtesy Ted Michel)

13

MORRIS MYSTERIES

There are mysteries which men can only guess at, which age by age they may solve only in part. --Bram Stoker

The Missing Morris Records

With the initial research on B.N. Morris in the 1980s, speculation began as to what became of the company's records. Knowing the company's office survived the fire provides a ray of hope to those wishing to discover logbooks, ledgers, or card-files that could tie the serial number of a boat to its original build-information. Letters written to Morris have been found in attics far from Veazie, Maine, fanning these Flames of Hope.

The Kennebec-Morris Hybrid

The Kennebec Boat and Canoe Company produced canoes and boats at their Waterville, Maine, factory between December 1909 and 1941. Their canoes are clearly marked with a metal Kennebec tag and serial number and some may also have a serial number tamped into the stem. The records of the Kennebec Company are among the very few existing records of canoe-builders from this time period, and can be accessed through Serial Number Search in the Forums on the website of the Wooden Canoe Heritage Association. These records hold no explanation as to why some Kennebec canoes were built with the splayed stem of a Morris; most Kennebec canoes have a narrow stem. Because records exist connecting a Kennebec serial number to a shipping date, it is known that these "hybrid" canoes appear during the years that both Kennebec and Morris were in production, essentially 1910 to 1920.

It has been speculated that these splayed-stem hulls might have originated at the Morris factory and were possibly sold to Kennebec whenever the latter couldn't keep up with orders. Another thought involves Kennebec employees who had once worked for Morris and learned the Morris-way of building a canoe. Kennebec Company founder, George F. Terry, was a businessman and not a canoe builder; he may have given employees some free rein when it came to building canoes, as it wasn't his field of expertise.

I had the opportunity to examine Kennebec 3365, which was shipped July 6, 1910, and compare it to a Morris c. 1915. I found the profile of the Kennebec to be different from the Morris, lending greater credence to the theory that someone at the Kennebec plant learned canoe-crafting at the factory in Veazie, and Mr. Terry didn't mind that not all stems on Kennebec canoes were uniform.

A puzzler to this particular story arose when canoe 3365 went into David Osborn's shop for repairs. With the top-cap of the closed gunwale system removed, Dave found numbers that could be 8287 tamped into the inwale. In our current Morris dating-system, this would indicate a shipping date of 1911—which isn't far-off the canoe's documented shipping date of 1910. This is a sponson canoe, however, and it's possible the inwale-number was a sponson's serial number.

Whether Morris tamped serial numbers into the inwale of their unfinished hulls is unknown as of this writing. The serial number plate was one of the final things placed on a Morris, tacked on after the varnish dried and the canoe was ready to go out the door. Morris may have marked their hulls with a serial number in some way, and this inwale location, which would be covered-up by the top-cap of the rail system, is an interesting find; however, whether Kennebec 3365 or any other Kennebec canoe began its life at the Morris factory is unknown. We only know there are numbers on the inwale of a 1910 Kennebec sponson canoe that don't correlate with the serial number placed on its splayed, Morris-like stem.

Bow stem of Kennebec 3365 (courtesy Shannon Abbott Henige)

Numbers tamped into inwale top of Kennebec 3365 (courtesy Dave Osborn)

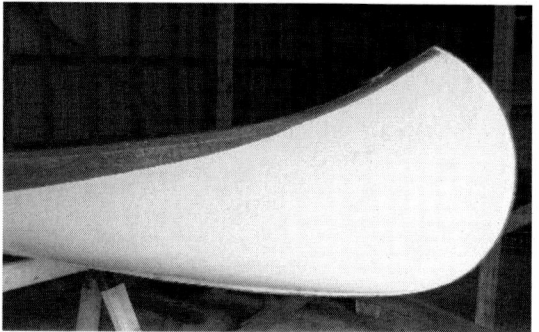

Profile of Kennebec 3365, a "Morris hybrid"

B.N. Morris profile for comparison (courtesy Michael Grace)

The Thirteen Morris Hulls Finished by Old Town

Within the repair records of Old Town Canoe are thirteen canoes labeled "B.N. Morris" that were shipped from June of 1921 to March of 1922. This information was discovered in the process of investigating the Old Town records for the purpose of scanning them for historical research. The records are that of Morris hulls finished in the Old Town shops. It has been speculated they were salvaged from the Morris factory fire, although it has also been suggested they could have been constructed after the fire. Newspaper accounts of the fire conflict as to what might have been saved. The *Bangor Daily Commercial* states, "...nearly all the canoes that were on hand were a total loss" while the *Bangor Daily News* contends that "Nearly all the finished canoes on hand were saved...". These thirteen hulls have serial numbers that are within the Morris numbering system and constitute the highest known Morris serial numbers.

In order of their serial numbers, these canoes are as follows:

16946, Old Town repair scan 527, shipped 10-21-21
16984, Old Town repair scan 525, shipped 6-24-21
17146, Old Town repair scan 523, shipped 6-29-21
17181, Old Town repair scan 521, shipped 6-29-21
17190, Old Town repair scan 519, shipped 6-20-21
17192, Old Town repair scan 517, shipped 3-17-22
17201, Old Town repair scan 515, shipped 9-14-21
17224, Old Town repair scan 513, shipped 9-14-21
17228, Old Town repair scan 511, shipped 6-20-21
17239, Old Town repair scan 507, shipped 6-29-21
17245, Old Town repair scan 509, shipped 6-17-21
17251, Old Town repair scan 505, shipped 8-25-21
17263, Old Town repair scan 503, shipped 6-28-21

Twelve of these canoes were shipped to individuals and one is simply designated "B.N. Morris". It would be interesting to know if these canoes were advertised and sold after completion or if they fulfilled orders. Each is finished differently as though to a specific order, but it seems unlikely the orders would date to a time prior to the fire.

None of these canoes has been reported to the Morris database, so it's possible none survive today. One existing Morris submitted to the database has a serial number that falls within this group of numbers. Morris 17103 was either shipped from the Morris factory prior to the fire, pulled from the fire as a finished canoe that needed no restoration at Old Town, or built and shipped separately from the group of thirteen. The fact of its existence suggests its hull was constructed around the same time as the hulls finished at Old Town.

It is unknown when, how, or if Morris marked their hulls with a serial number prior to the brass plate that went onto a varnished inwale or stem. If this group of thirteen hulls constitutes Morris fire survivors, the fact that they were assigned serial numbers suggests Morris put a number someplace on their hulls prior to final finishing. It would be interesting to know if the serial numbers on the group of thirteen are tamped into the stems or if the numbers appear on a metal plate. Perhaps the plate itself was attached to the canoe early-on, removed while the interior was varnished, and then replaced. Any one of these thirteen canoes might have much to say to us.

The Post-fire Morris Canoes

Bert Morris was building canoes "more for a hobby" following the factory fire. We know from his contact with Joe Seliga that he produced a brochure showing three models. It may be assumed he was using forms that survived the fire and that these post-fire canoes might be similar in appearance to the easily-recognized Morris canoe—in thirty years, Bert made only minor changes in the appearance of his basic canoe. Perhaps he changed the canoe enough to make any that survive UFOs (unidentified floating objects), or maybe he produced so few that none exist today. Did the canoes Bert Morris built in the 1930s have open gunwales and hardwood stems? Perhaps eventually some will come out of hiding.

The Middle Names

What did the **N** in **Bert N. Morris** stand for? As of this writing, I have no confirmed answer. Bert's maternal grandmother's maiden name was **Nelson**, but **Bert Nelson Morris** is only a guess. A name isn't filled in on his birth record. I'd also like to know if **Bert** is the diminutive of a grander name, such as **Albert**. **Albert Nelson Morris** slides off the tongue a bit more easily than **Bert Nelson Morris**. As with other loose ends in the Morris story, I plan to dig more. Bert's baptismal record would be a nice find. He was born in Bangor, and if Christened there, any record may have gone up in smoke when the Bangor Fire of 1911 swept through town. I've thought **Charles A. Morris** was possibly Charles **Albion** Morris, but have found nothing to confirm this. Charlie was born in Bangor—again, that "fire wall".

The Old Town Canoe Ordered by Morris

SHIPPED 4/2⅞ 1919. Canoe No. 53128
To Morris Canoe Co. Our Order No. 722
  Vezie, Maine Your Order No. 7

Via M.C.R.R.

Length	16	Half Built	JAN 11 1919
Grade	CS Model HW	Completed	JAN 11 1919
Planking	WC	Oiled	JAN 13 1919
Gunwales	Spruce	Canvassed	JAN 14 1919
Decks	Maple	Filled	JAN 14 1919
Thwarts	"	Stored	
Seats	"	2nd Filled	FEB 7 1919
Half Ribs		Stored	
Finish Rails		Railed	MAR 4 1919 Ingalls
Keel	MAR 4 1919	Fitted	MAR 5 1919
O. S. Stems		Colored	MAR 6 1919
Floor Rack		Varnished	MAR 3 1919
Sponsons		Stored	
Color	D. Green		

    The records of Old Town Canoe contain this build record, showing a dark green, 16 foot, CS (common sense, or second) grade HW model canoe with red Western cedar planking, closed spruce gunwales, and maple decks, thwarts, and seat frames that was sent to the Morris Canoe Company in April of 1919.

Event Timeline

1835 Samuel Laine Fish moves from Leeds to Veazie, builds a house

1856 Twenty name changes from Fish to Morris

1860 Charles Morris born, February 10

1861 Albion Morris enlists in Maine 2d as a Musician, February 10

1866 Bert Morris born, June 24

1879 Samuel Fish Morris dies in Veazie

1880s Shop building erected behind barn on Flagg St

1888 Charlie's daughter born

1889 First mention in print of B.N. Morris canoes, July 6

1889 Maine Register lists Albion as carpenter, Chas as carriage maker; EH Gerrish listed as maker of "canoes, boats, and paddles" in Bangor

1890 National ad campaign begins—several ads in *Forest and Stream*

1891 Ad in *Forest and Stream* indicating L.W. Ferdinand of Boston is Morris agent; Ferdinand offers Morris canoes in their catalog

1891 State Street property purchased

1892 B.N. Morris Factory built on State Street for $3,000

1892 B.N. Morris has 6 employees

1892 Morris exhibits canvas boats and canoes in Boston at MA Charitable Mechanic Association; wins bronze medal

1893-1897 Economic depression, Rushton's wider marketing efforts fall on hard times

1893 Charlie listed as officer in Veazie Grange

1893 First Morris catalog; Indian canoe is among 15 vessels

1893 World's Columbian Exposition: Morris displays 6 canvas boats and canoes, May 1-Oct 30

1893 Charlie's wife Gracie dies, October 31

1896 Albion Morris dies, October 2

1898 First use of Morris canoe image that would become WCHA logo

1898 Bert marries Ella Page, October 15

1900 Sequential serial numbering begins-- oval inwale tag; canoe has 2 pair cants

1900 Indian Old Town Canoe begins business

1901 Charles Morris listed in city directory as "Machinist for BN Morris Canoe"

1902 Expansion made to factory, cost $1500

1902 B.N. Morris has 25 employees

1902 Rushton wood-canvas Indian Girl directly competes

1903 Canoe 1876 no. 94 first grade canoe, Special Indian, shipped June 6th

1903 City of Veazie votes to move hydrant on Mill St to State St. "in front of BN Morris Canoe Co."

1905 Last ads for Special Indian models

1905 Chestnut Canoe Company of New Brunswick patents wood-canvas canoe construction

1905 (about) Morris 2972, 2 pair cant ribs

1905 (about) **Veazie** canoe, no number (two holes inwale), 2 pair cant ribs

1905 (about) Morris 3013, 3 pair cant ribs

1905 Sophronia Morris dies, December 12

Model A-D begins—all B.N. Morris canoes are first grade

1906 CJ Molitor becomes Morris dealer

1908 Veazie Canoe Company is incorporated; appears in Maine Annual reports of Bureau of Taxation and Assessment

1908 Ford introduces the Model T

1909 EH Gerrish sells his canoe business

1909 Kennebec Canoe Co. founded in Waterville, ME, December

1910 Morris serial number plate moves from inwale to bow stem

1911 Kennedy Bros. (Minneapolis) receipt for canoes with serial numbers 7969, 7974, 8307, 8435

1912 receipt for Morris 9456 shipped April 9; Morris 9023 shipped May 15

1913 Kennedy Bros. (Minneapolis) sells Veazie 716 (it has curved deck)

1914 first curved deck appears on BN Morris canoe

1917 Last heart-shaped deck—all new Morris canoes have curved deck

1917 Ella Page Morris dies at age 41, January 30

1917 U.S. enters WWI, April 6

1917 Bert Morris marries Margaret Pierce, October 23

1918 B.N. Morris is incorporated, February 6

1918 WWI ends, November 11

1919 U.S. Government imposes tax of 10% on Sporting Goods; Morris increases catalog prices 25%

1919 Morris orders CS grade HW from Old Town, April

1919 Fire destroys Morris factory, December 15

1920 Census taken January 15&16 lists Bert Morris as "canvas canoe manufacturer" and Charles as "machinist in canoe shop"

1920 City of Veazie votes to not tax Bert Morris if he rebuilds factory

1921 CJ Molitor orders livery canoes from Old Town Canoe

1921-22 Morris hulls finished at Old Town are shipped to buyers

1922 CJ Molitor closes canoe livery

1923 Bert Morris is treasurer of Morris-Lancaster Co., dealers in Paige and Jewett automobiles, September 7

1928 Charles Morris dies at age 68, May 9

1929 Stock market crashes; the Great Depression begins

1930 Bert Morris listed as having no occupation in 1930 Census

1938 Joe Seliga writes Bert Morris and receives reply stating that Bert builds canoes only as a hobby

1940 Bert Morris dies in his Veazie home, age 73, May 31

1941 Kennebec Canoe Company ceases business

1950 Margaret Morris dies

2014 Morris Database Statistics

I have two canvas-covered canoes, both old and beautifully made. They came from the Penobscot River in Maine long ago, and I treasure them for the tradition of craftsmanship in their construction, a pride not only of form and line but of everything that went into their building. When I look at modern canoes, of metal or fiberglass stamped out like so many identical coins, I cherish mine even more ...
--Sigurd F. Olson

In 2007, Denis Kallery and I began collecting information on Morris canoes and boats to see what they might tell us. As of December 15, 2014, there are **331** entries in the B.N. Morris Database of the Wooden Canoe Heritage Association. In some cases, information on a canoe is sketchy—consisting only of a serial number and deck-type; in other cases, we obtained precise details and pictures; therefore, database statistics provided here cannot thoroughly represent the canoes on the list but they do provide a picture.

Included in the database is information from the repair records of Old Town Canoe: 13 Morris hulls finished and shipped from Old Town in 1921-22 and another 12 Morris canoes that were repaired at Old Town. None of these canoes has been reported as existing today, but information on them is detailed and helps us understand Morris production.

Five of the canoes listed in Jill and Jeff Dean's 1985 *Wooden Canoe* article have been reported to the database and their information fleshed-out, but the others exist in the database as serial numbers alone. It can be assumed that since these canoes were in the hands of WCHA members in 1985, they possibly still exist. Also included in the database is information on Morris canoes collected by the late Dave Baker.

Three canoes in the database count are known not to exist, as information on them was provided prior to a Viking funeral. Some of their parts will live on, however, in other Morris canoes.

Of the canoes with serial numbers, **69** is the lowest number and **17263** the highest. Neither canoe may currently exist, as both numbers were found among repair records at Old Town. Morris 17263 was among the 13 canoes discussed in "Morris Mysteries" and Morris 69 was sent to Old Town for repair in 1942.

Morris **70** is the lowest serial-numbered existing Morris in the database and the one with the best example of Decal Version 2 (see image p. 108). Morris **17103** has the highest serial number of the canoes known to exist. There is one Morris Double End Canvas Rowing Boat, number 158.

Veazie Canoes

12 is the total number of Veazie Canoe Company Canoes

1 is currently in Ireland

2 have a keyhole deck; tack holes on inwale

10 have a rectangular serial number plate on the bow stem

3 have mahogany decks and maple thwarts and seat frames; in one case, the mahogany deck is heart-shaped, leading me to suspect Morris used whatever was handy on some Veazie canoes.

Veazie 1101 has the highest serial number and is the only Veazie canoe with open gunwales

6—16 footers

2—17 footers

B.N. Morris Canoes Without Serial Numbers

14 have two cant rib pairs and no sign of ever having had a serial number

20 reported with no information—the person reporting unable to examine the canoe for signs of tack holes or count cant ribs

9 have tack holes on the inwale

7 have tack holes on the stem

1 has a metal tag "B.N. Morris/Builder/Veazie, ME"

3 have a metal tag "From/The Morris/Canoe Factory/Veazie Maine"

B.N. Morris Canoes With Serial Numbers

8 have two cant-rib pairs (initially, I didn't ask for cant-rib counts, so this number may not reflect all database canoes with two pairs of cants)

45 have an oval plate on the inwale

22 have a rectangular serial number plate rotated to vertical position (c.1912-1916)

102 have a rectangular serial number plate on bow stem in horizontal position

5 have a rectangular plate on the bow seat

B.N. Morris Canoes (with and without serial numbers)

14 have decals

4 have Abercrombie&Fitch tags

5 have Folsom Arms tags

3 have sponsons

4 have sail rigs

27 are open gunwale—numbers beginning c.1912

1—12 footer

4—13 footers

11—15 footers

53—16 footers

88—17 footers

42—18 footers

2—20 footers

4—Molitors (36 inch bow deck/24 inch stern deck)

3—48 inch decks both ends

Morris 15288 is an 18 foot Model A type 3 canoe with 48 inch decks (courtesy Ken Kelly)

Lady and Tiger is one of four Molitors in the Morris Database (courtesy Ken Kelly)

Morris 14964 is a 17 foot, Model A type 3, open gunwale canoe with Special Ends; *Tsigana* is discussed in *Wooden Canoe* issue 27. (courtesy Scottie Baker)

Morris 15883 is a type 1 canoe with curved decks, seen also p.7 (courtesy Dave McDaniel)

Companies and Materials Used by Morris

Morris receipts from 1911-12

A file of invoices found in the former Morris home by its present owner sheds light on individuals and companies doing business with B.N. Morris in the years 1909-1912. Receipts contained in a file box labeled "12" may represent all of B.N. Morris Company's bills for 1911-12. Another stack of receipts represents a portion of 1909-10. At the time these bills were generated, B.N. Morris had been in business twenty years and had numerous established contacts. These invoices indicate that Morris utilized several different providers offering the same type of merchandise, suggesting he looked for the best deal.

These century-old documents involve interesting graphics in addition to the information they contain, so are shared here as images rather than a simple list. Due to the quantity of material, those items that may be of most interest have been selected—along with those that might bring a smile. They appear here in no particular order-- based in some cases on what fits the page-- with an attempt to group items from providers of like-kind. Most images have been cropped to increase the size of the important portion of the document.

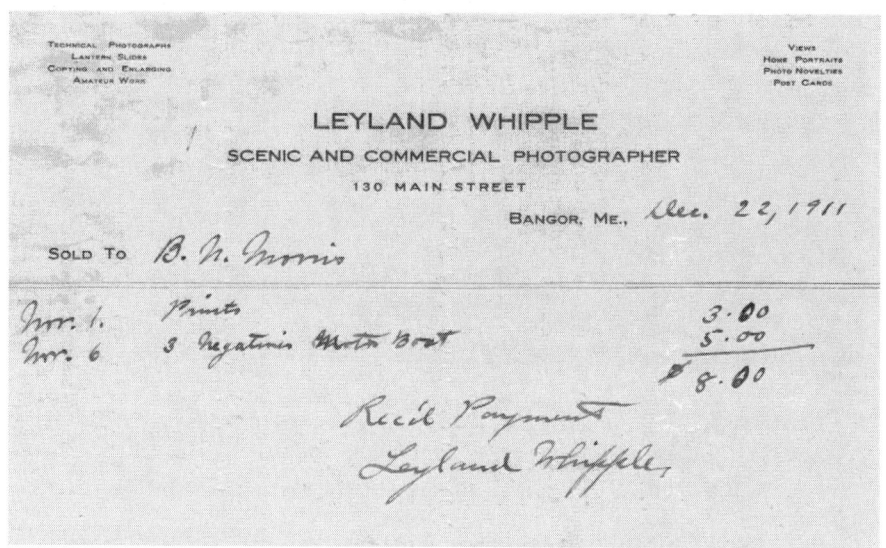

Invoice for photos taken of the Morris Motor Boat

Invoice for printer's cuts needed for adding images to catalogs and advertising

Invoice to "Retouch and engrave 2 halftones/top and side views of canoe"

Invoice for exhibition space in New York City's Hudson Terminal Building, which was an office skyscraper built to serve the Hudson Terminal, a station on the Hudson and Manhattan Railroad in Lower Manhattan. It was demolished to make way for the World Trade Center.

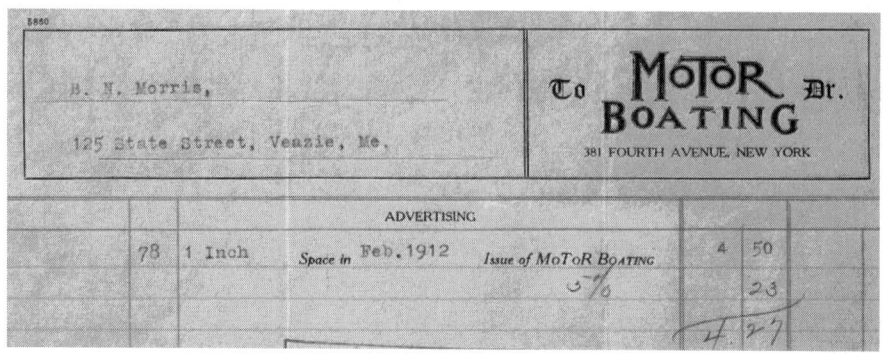
Invoice for ad in *Motor Boating* magazine

Cost of an ad placed in a canoe club's minstrel program

Invoice may be for tags such as that below

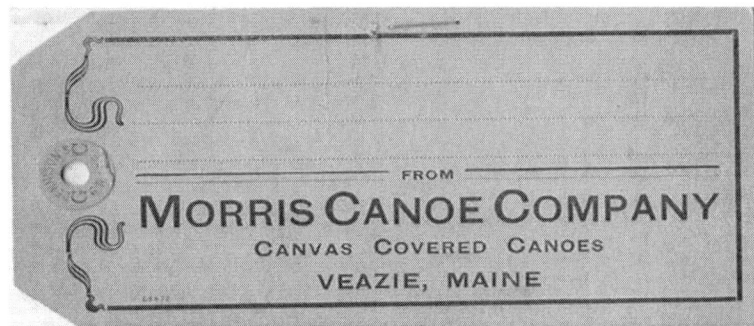

Morris shipping tag (courtesy Louis King)

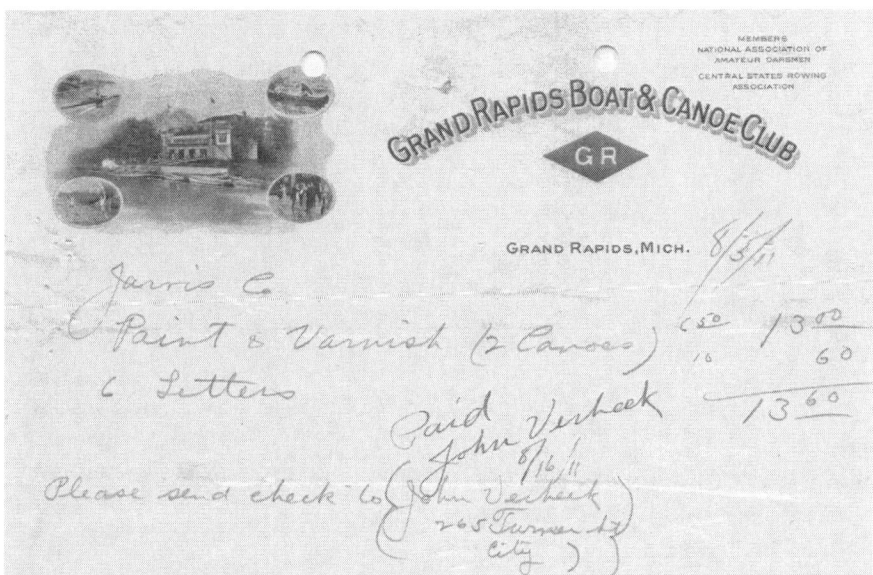

Invoice for work done on canoes that arrived at the Grand Rapids dealership with damage. Notation near bottom is believed to have been made by Bert Morris.

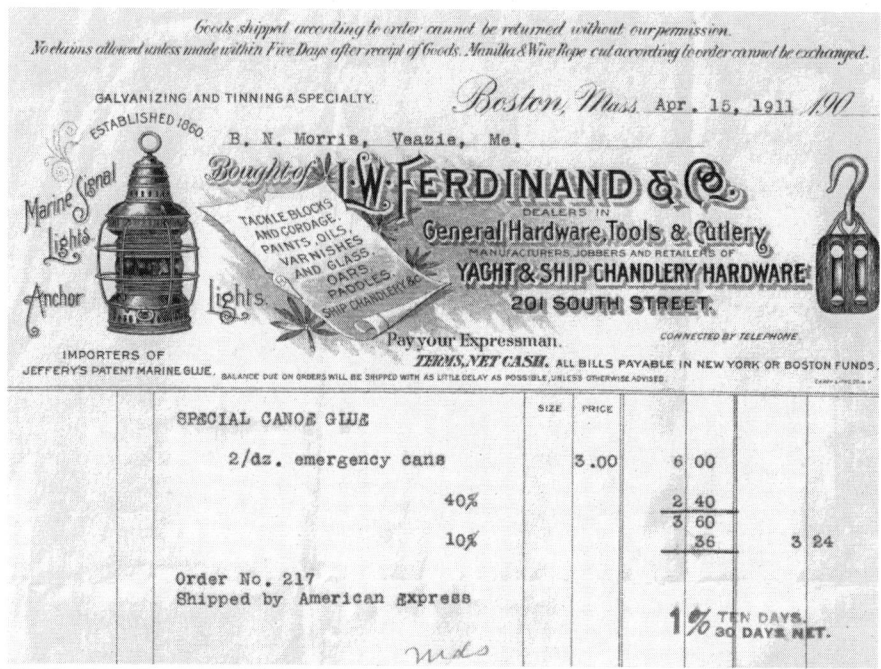

L.W. Fredinand was Morris's first agent and possibly provided some of the items that, by 1911, Morris purchased from other companies. This and the receipt below represent the only communications with Ferdinand in these 1909-1912 receipts.

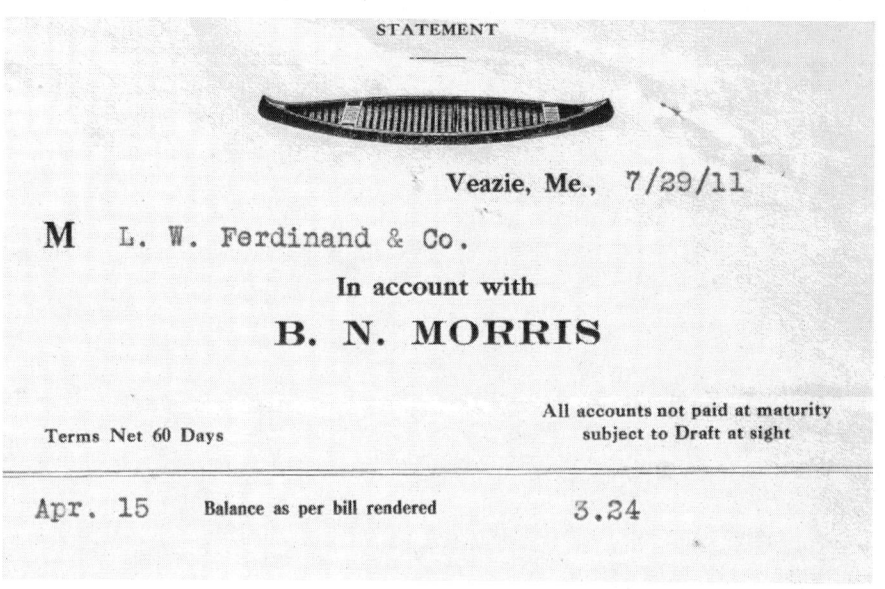

Bills from Sherwin-Williams during the 1910-12 period are substantial, yet there is also an occasional invoice from Wadsworth. Their paint chip examples are displayed on p.115.

The majority of purchases from Wadsworth, Howland Co. in this time period involve solvents and the following brushes: 2" ox hair, 2" badger hair, 3" dbl. thick badger hair, 4" Wang Wall Brush, 4" My Dollar Brush, 2 ½" C.H. Peerless Color Brush, and 4" O.K. Stucco Brush. Wadsworth, Howland Company produced the paint samples on p. 115 that date to 1905, but considering the number of Sherwin-Williams receipts, it is obvious that by 1911 they were Morris's main paint supplier. There are, however, receipts from several other suppliers of varnish, shellac, lead, silex and various solvents indicating that Morris shopped around for paints and components of their filler recipe. In some cases they were provided products gratis, seemingly as an incentive to do business.

Colors listed on multiple Sherwin-Williams invoices are as follows: QD Brilliant Green, Mohawk Red, Ex Coach Green Lt, Ex Coach Green Dk, Metalastic Ext Pure White, White Rough Stuff, Red Rough Stuff, Brt Sienna, Orinoco Verm'l, Auto Gray, Canoe Gray, Free Flow Gray, Chro Yellow, CP Terra Cotta, Ivy Green, Fern Leaf Green, Yale Blue, Bay Brown, and Semi Gloss Yacht White. Morris also obtained Canoe Spar Varnish from Sherwin-Williams.

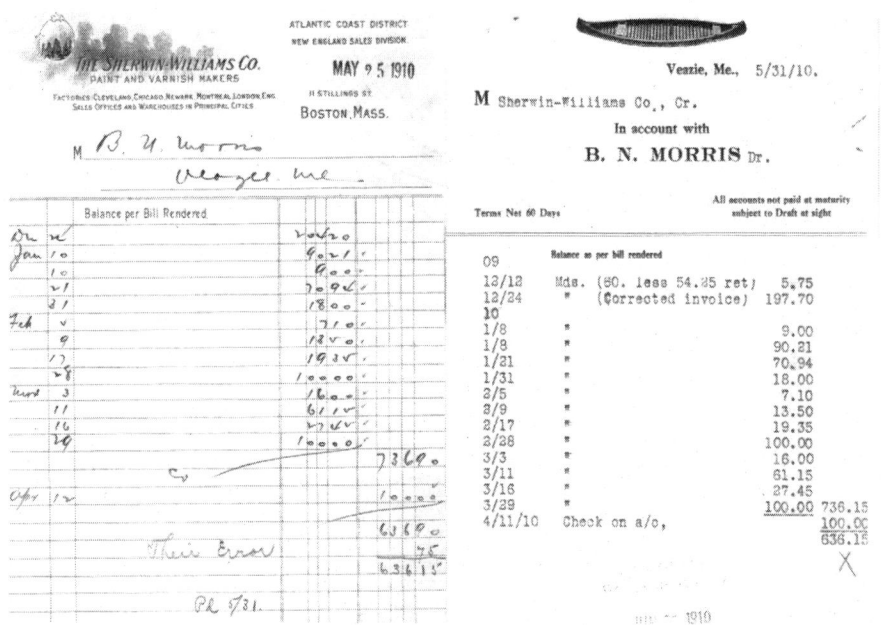

Invoice for $636.15 in paint ordered over a period of four months. Note that Morris checks the math and a corresponding invoice on B.N. Morris stationery is typed out. Notations on the original invoice are believed to be in Bert's handwriting.

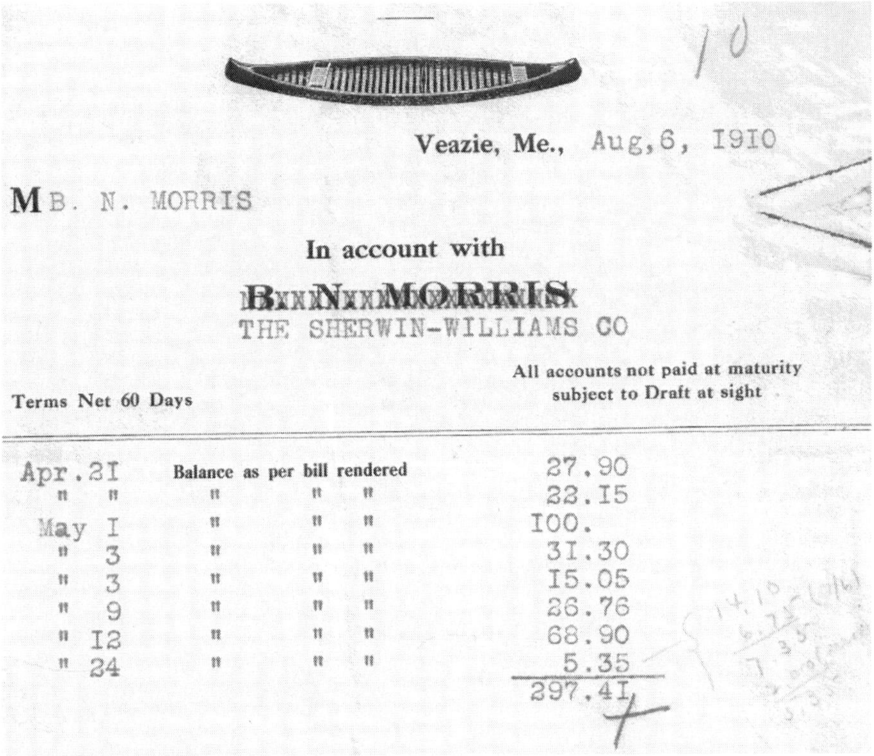

Veazie, Me., Aug,6, 1910

MB. N. MORRIS

In account with

B. N. MORRIS

THE SHERWIN-WILLIAMS CO

Terms Net 60 Days

All accounts not paid at maturity subject to Draft at sight

Apr. 21	Balance as per bill rendered	27.90
" "	" " "	22.15
May 1	" " "	100.
" 3	" " "	31.30
" 3	" " "	15.05
" 9	" " "	26.76
" 12	" " "	68.90
" 24	" " "	5.35
		297.41

Paint orders for April and May of 1910, with additional orders added at the right in what is believed to be Bert Morris's handwriting.

ATLANTIC COAST DISTRICT
NEW ENGLAND SALES DIVISION

THE SHERWIN-WILLIAMS CO.
PAINT AND VARNISH MAKERS

FACTORIES: CLEVELAND, CHICAGO, NEWARK, MONTREAL, LONDON, ENG.
SALES OFFICES AND WAREHOUSES IN PRINCIPAL CITIES.

11 STILLINGS ST., BOSTON 4/21/10

SOLD TO B. N. Morris
Veazie, Maine

MC RR — 02378

ORDER — SLIP NO. — TERMS 60 DAYS

5 - lbs	Brt Sienna in Oil	5Pc	.14	.70
15 "	Yale Blue in Japan D	5Pc)		
10 "	" " " " L	5Pc)	.35	8.75
25 "	Mohawk Red Ground in Japan 5Pc)			
5 "	Orinoco Vernm'l " "	5Pc)	.34	10.20
10 "	Auto Gray in Japan D	5s	.25	2.50
				$22.15

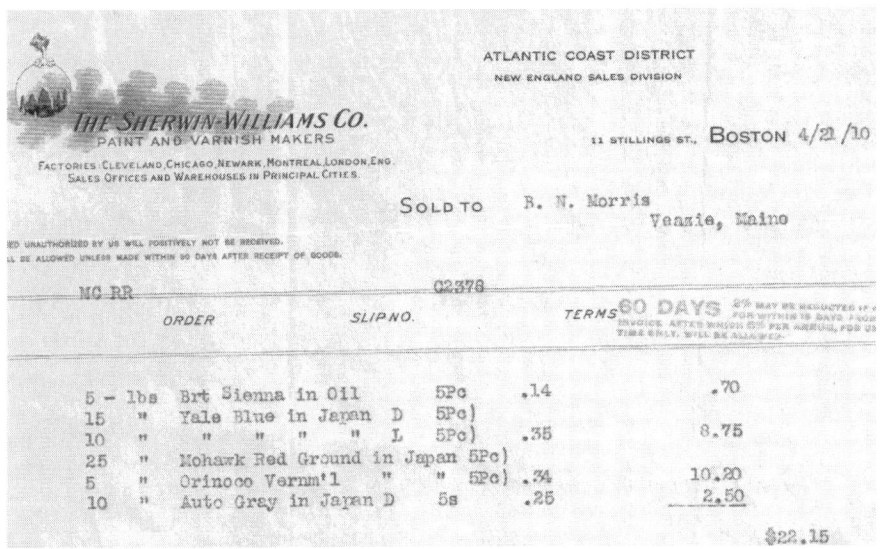

Sherwin-Williams: Covering the Earth since 1866 and covering Morris canoes in 1910

   **B. N. MORRIS**

OARS, PADDLES
CANOE FITTINGS

TELEGRAPH ADDRESS
VEAZIE

BUILDER OF

CANVAS CANOES
CANVAS MOTOR BOATS

HULLS OR COMPLETE
EQUIPMENT

CABLE ADDRESS
MORRIS, BANGOR

VEAZIE, MAINE. April 22, 1912.

The Sherwin-Williams Co.
    Boston, Mass.

Gentlemen;-

        I am inclosing herewith check for $545.48 in settlement of account to March 1st, as requested in your favor of the 20th.

        Very truly yours,

LWJ.
        B. N. MORRIS.

Note that by 1912, Morris is using images other than the Special Indian on their paperwork

TRADE MARK
BUNKER HILL
VARNISHES
ESTABLISHED 1825

Burbank & Ryder Varnish Co.
VARNISH AND JAPAN MAKERS.
62 ALFORD STREET, CHARLESTOWN DISTRICT.

Boston
July 24-11

Sold to B. N. Morris,
    Veazie, Me.

TERMS

SHIPPED BY

1½ Gal Durable Spar	@ $1 85		
1½ Gal Special Spar	@ $1 75	Gratis	

One of several companies supplying Morris with varnish; note "gratis"

HARRISON BROS. & CO., INC.
OF BOSTON
PAINT COLORS VARNISH WHITE LEAD CHEMICALS
112 PEARL STREET
BOSTON 10/13/11

SOLD TO B. N. Morris,
Veazie, Maine.

Order No. 5680
Your Order No. 308
Shipped by Fgt.
Terms 60-2%-15d
F. O. B. Boston

307

	QUANTITY	PRICE	GROSS AMOUNT	NET AMOUNT	PACKAGES	TOTAL
5/100 Pure Lead O	500 Lbs.	.07¼				$36.25
5 Kegs						
FS 5722						

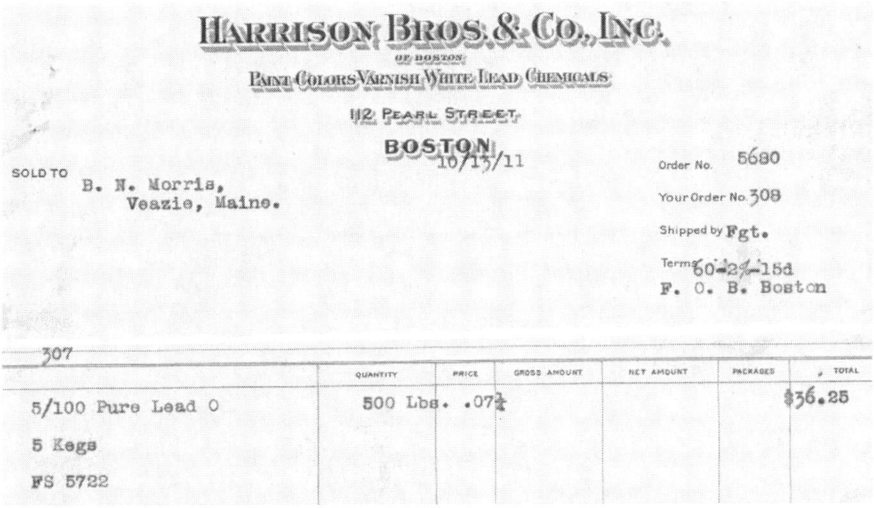

Lead is a component of the filler used to treat canvas, preventing mold and mildew

Meter Reading June 28 9320 K. W. Hrs. 1911
Last " 7740 "
Amount current used 1580 "at ... cts. per K. W. Hr. less
"at 15 cts. " " "
"at 16 cts. " " "
MINIMUM CHARGE
Balance
10% discount on meter bills if paid by July 10
POSITIVELY NO DISCOUNT ALLOWED AFTER THIS DATE
Total 13.64

BANGOR RAILWAY AND ELECTRIC CO., In account with

B N MORRIS

VEAZIE ME

Received Payment JUL 10 1911 Bangor Railway & Electric Co.
PER

We reserve the right to discontinue Service if Bills are overdue
Bring this Bill for settlement

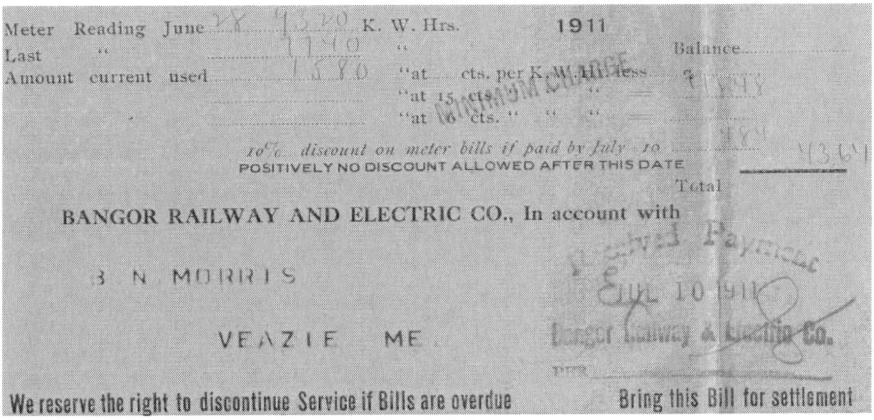

One of many electric bills

GASOLINE AND NAPHTHA NOT SOLD FOR ILLUMINATING PURPOSES IN BUILDINGS.

YOUR ORDER No.
TERMS NET CASH.

Standard Oil Co. of New York.
BOSTON DEPARTMENT.

No. 4678
1169

Bangor, Me. AUG 26 1910 190

Sold to B. N. Morris

Shipped via Veazie

WHEN WE DELIVER GOODS TO TRANSPORTATION COMPANIES IN GOOD ORDER, AND TAKE THEIR RECEIPT OUR RESPONSIBILITY CEASES

50 Gals Motor Gasoline 13½ 6.75

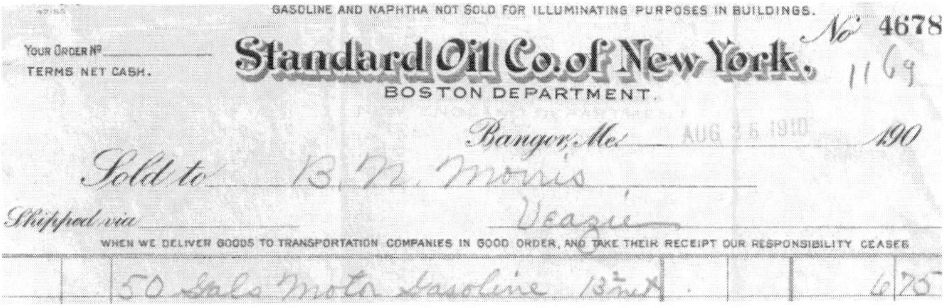

Invoice for “Motor Gasoline”, possibly for the Motor Boat

One of many invoices from several companies supplying Morris with goods related to the Motor Boat he promoted around 1910-12. This company is in Motor City (Detroit).

Invoice for parts related to the Morris Motor Boat

Morris Motor Boat (courtesy *The Historic Wood Canoe and Boat Manufacturer Catalog Collection* edited by Daniel Miller and Benson Gray)

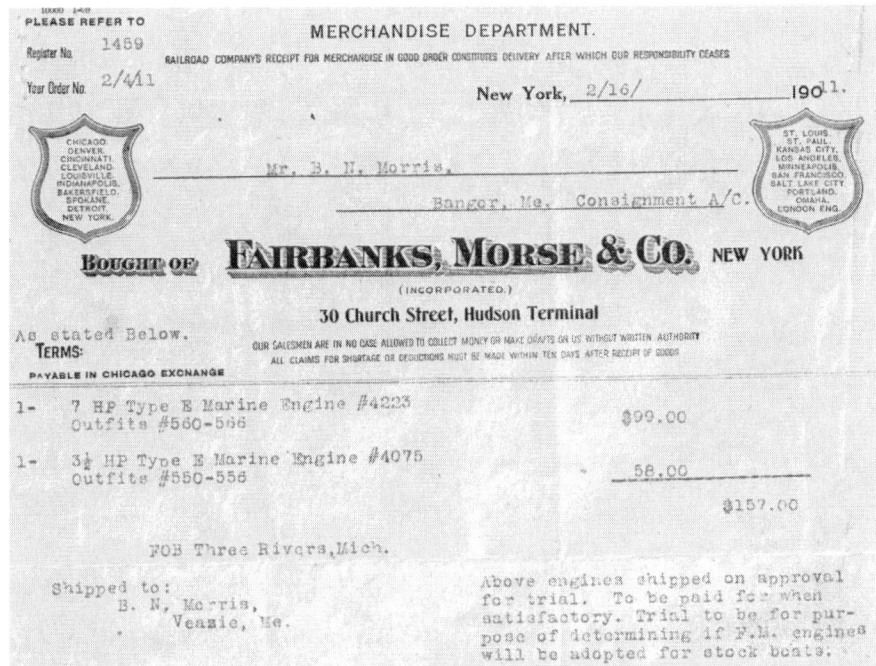

Invoice for two engines; Morris Motor Boat with 3 HP engine sold for $225 and is advertised as traveling at 9 miles per hour.

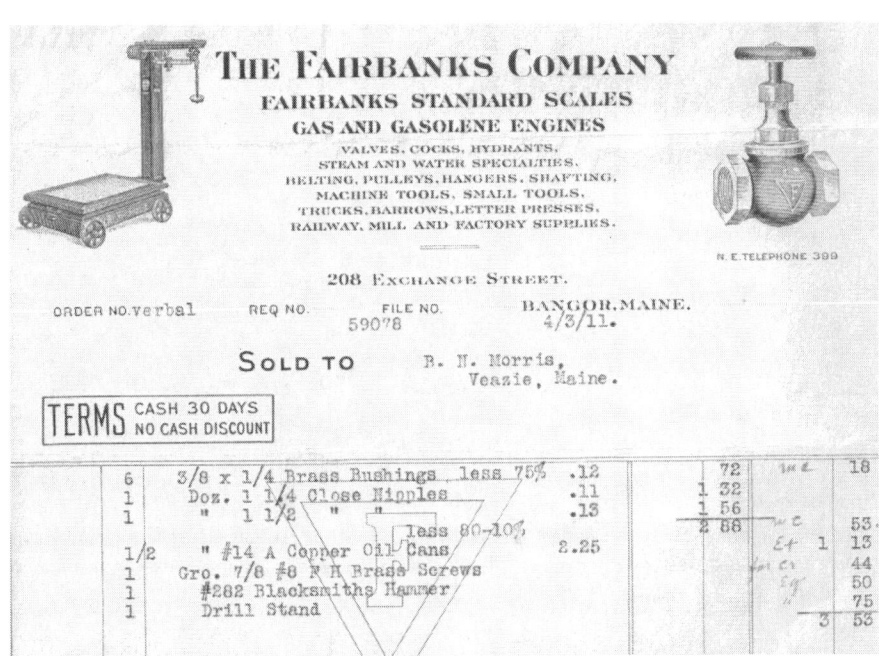

Beaver Manufacturing Company

AUTO & MARINE GASOLINE MOTORS

Codes Used: Liebers and Western Union
Cable Address: "BEAVER MILWAUKEE"

MAIN OFFICE AND WORKS
CHASE & BURRELL STS.

Milwaukee, Oct. 13, 1911

TERMS: paid
OUR ORDER NO. 7964
YOUR ORDER NO. Verbal

SOLD TO B N MORRIS BANGOR MAINE
Shipped to VEAZIE MAINE
SHIPPED VIA G T c/o M C at Auburn, Me.

1	TB Marine Motor No. 1838 - RH - End Lugs		100 00	
	1¼" Schebler Carburetor			
	Maximus Timer		3 00	103 00
	Comb Water & Oil Pump			
	6 Lead Force Feed Oiler			
	Starting Crank			
	Special Crank Shaft - see sketch			
"	16" Cone FW - see sketch			
"	Exhaust Pipe - lowest point not lower than crank case			
"	Aluminum TA-199 Intake Pipe			
	T-3-B Cylinder - end lug			
	Crank Shaft with starting end 15/16 x 4			

OCT 16 1911

BEAVER MFG. CO. PAID OCT 16

Warehouses:
Chicago, Ill.
Boston, Mass.
St. Paul, Minn.

John A. Dunn Company,
Chairs & Rattan Products
Gardner, Mass.

Established 1889.
Incorporated 1902.
Cable Address "Chairman"
Codes:
A.B.C. Western Union
Liebers.

INVOICE NO. 833
TERMS
SOLD TO Mr. B. N. Morris, Veazie, Me.

DEPARTMENT 3

May 25, 1910.

UPON THE DEATH, INSOLVENCY OR GENERAL ASSIGNMENT OF THE DEBTOR, OR UPON THE ENTRY OF ANY JUDGMENT AGAINST HIM, THE AMOUNT OF THIS INVOICE SHALL BE DUE AT ONCE.

YOUR ORDER	OUR ORDER	CAR		VIA			
57	4184	1	bale #1 common	M.C.	Came C. Pd.		
			Less 15%		46.00		
					6.90		
					39.10		
			Sacking @ .30		.30		39.40
			Frt. Rec. #3188. Frt. Prepaid.				
			1 bale.				

Invoice for a bale of cane suggests that Morris seats were caned at the factory or that Morris supplied materials to those who worked elsewhere, giving Morris greater control over cost.

BANGOR, ME., April 1, 1911

M

To A. J. INFIORATI Dr.
Signs and Show Cards of Every Description

SIGNS
In Wood, Cloth, Glass, Metal and Wire

46 CENTRAL STREET

WINDOW LETTERS
In Wood, Metal and Enamel

Date	Qty	Description	Amount
Dec 5		1 Stripe	1.75
Jan 11		2 " Canoe + 1 Motor Boat	5.50
" 31		Old Eng. B + 2 Stripes	3.00
Feb 10		2 gold + 1 paint stripe	3.75
" 14		2 " stripe + lettering	3.75
" 15		2 stripe	3.25
" 16	3	"	4.50
" 21	2	"	3.00
" 22	2	"	3.00
" 25	2	"	3.00
" 27	2	"	3.00
Mar 4	2	"	3.00
" 7	3	"	4.50
" 10	3	"	4.50
" 14	2	"	3.00
" 15	2	" Canoe + 1 Motor B.	6.00
" 16	2	" "	3.00
" 21	2	" " + 2 lettering	4.00
" 22	2	" " + 1 "	4.00
" 23	1	" " + 1 "	2.00
" 31	3	"	4.50
Apl 1	2	" 2 mon.	4.50

by cash Apl. 1, 25.00

B.N. Morris apparently didn't have a sign painter on staff but utilized the services of Mr. Infiorati of Bangor in this time period. Note that he decorated two Motor Boats and completed two or three canoes per day. It's interesting to see how common it was for canoes to be ordered with decoration. There are several pages like this in the receipts file. If the serial numbers of the canoes had been added, the information would have been even more valuable.

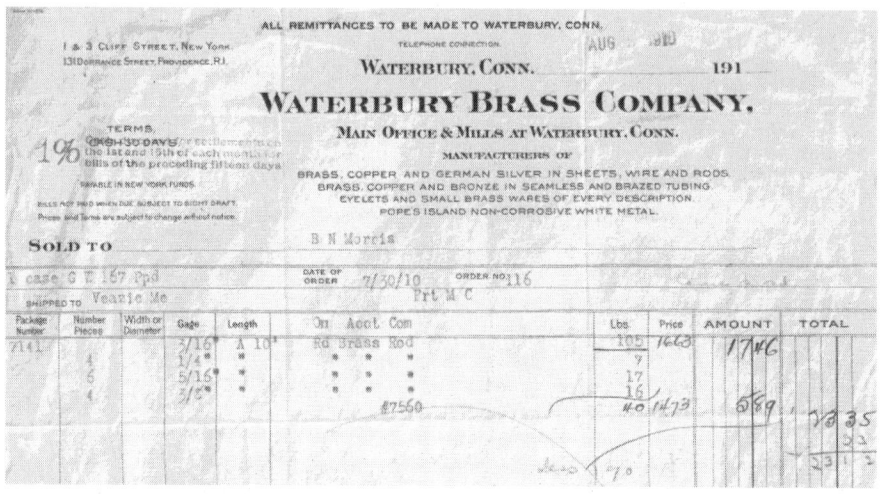

Waterbury was a major brass provider to B.N. Morris in this time period

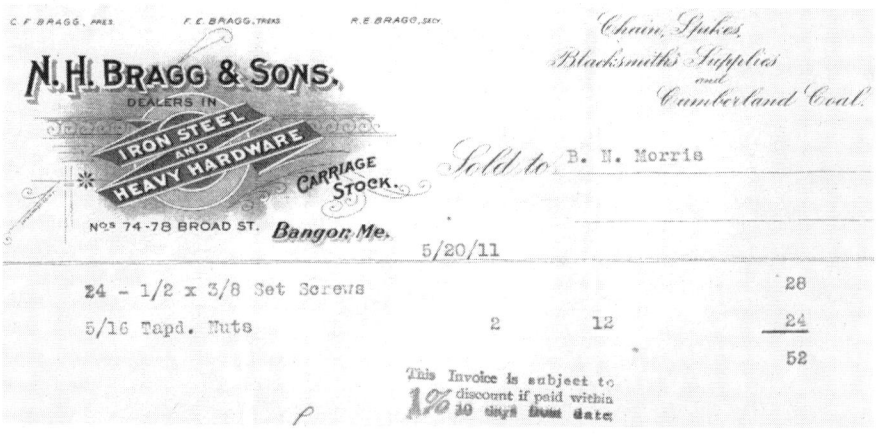

Invoice for nickel plating that includes flag pole sockets

U. T. HUNGERFORD BRASS & COPPER CO.

NEW YORK 1/4/12

IF ANY REPLY REFER TO BC 1/4

Mr. B.N. Morris,
Veazie,
Me.

Dear Sir;-
We are in receipt of your letter of the 26th ult. in regard to deuction of 7-1/2% on invoice Sept. 5th. You returned part of this invoice and we gave you credit for same under date of December 1st at the price same was charged at, hence we do not see how you are entitled to 7-1/2% on anything more than the amount you retained which amounts to $111.20.

We trust this will make this clear to you and soliciting your further favors, we remain,

Yours truly,

U.T.HUNGERFORD BRASS & COPPER CO.

BY:

Credit only where credit is due...

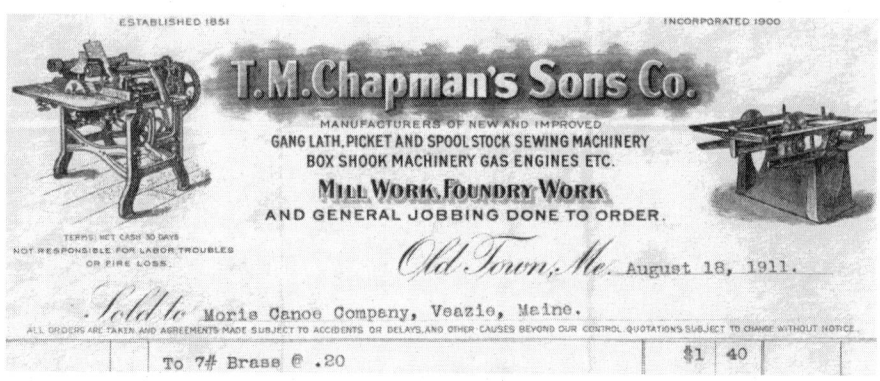

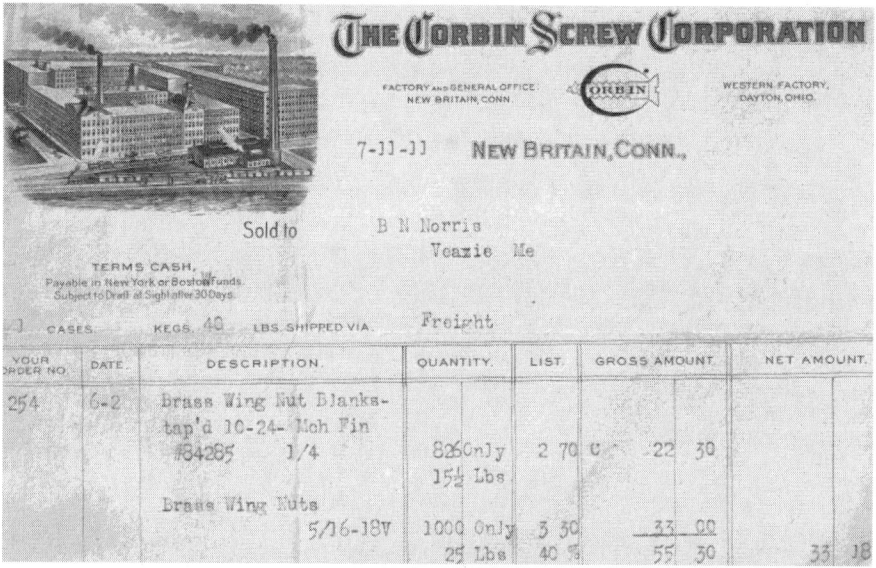

Reverse side of a Hungerford invoice lists what they provide

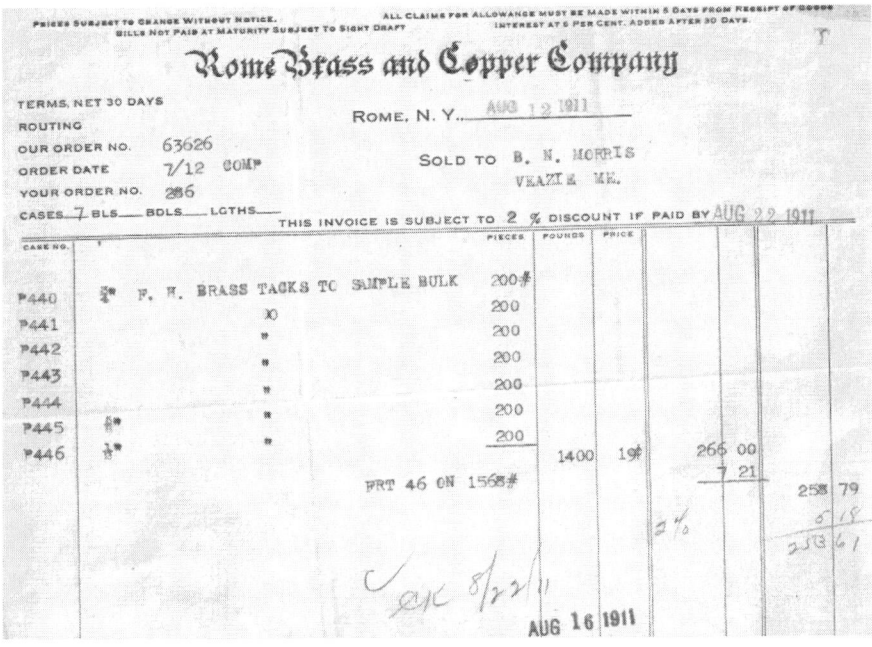

Brass tacks by the ton...

Example of wages paid an electrician

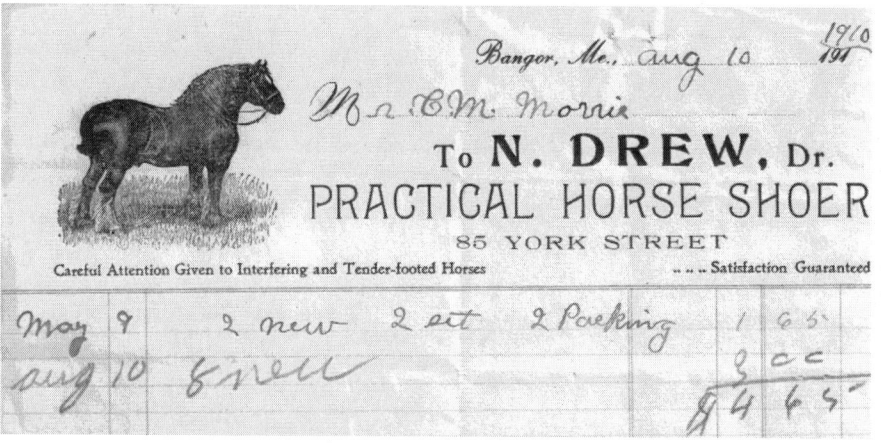

Above is a reminder that horses were used to move canoe-loads about; there are several invoices from the farrier and also bills for horse feed, suggesting that the horses were kept on-site. There is no mention of horses perishing in the factory fire.

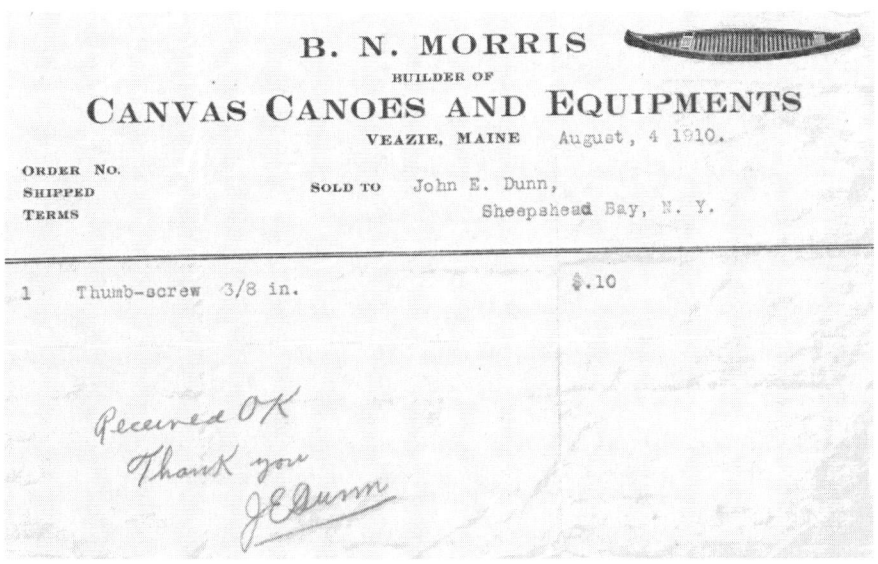

One of many bills for livestock feed

Invoice for a ten cent thumb screw, which was returned with payment and filed

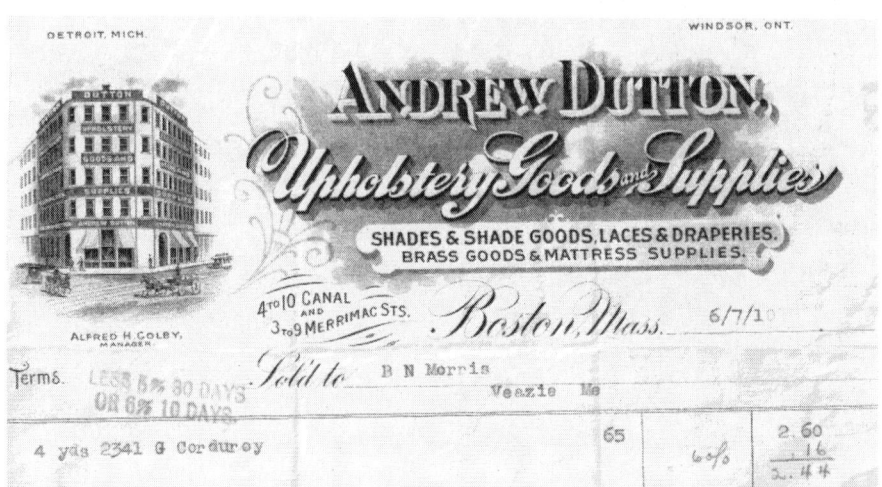

Morris offered a hair-filled cushion, covered in "heavy velour or best corduroy" and either had them made on-site or provided the materials for off-site manufacture.

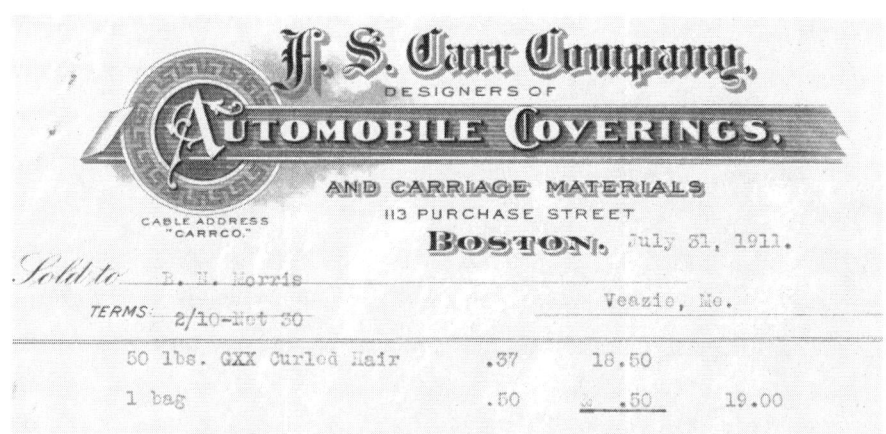

Invoice for horse hair that went inside the cushions

Invoice for burlap; canoes were packed in straw-filled burlap for shipping

B.N. Morris's sailmaker—6 canoe sails at $2.25 each

One of very few documents relating to the Veazie Canoe Company

Joseph B. Morrell *Cable Address: Calvert.* *Amos D. Carver*

ESTABLISHED 1827.

Baker, Carver & Morrell,
COTTON DUCK

#H 7197   71, 73 & 75 *Front Street,*

New York Oct. 6, 1911

Sold to   B.N. Morris, Veazie, Me.

Terms   CHECKED BY

```
10 rolls 54" #10 Cotton duck
    #32780-103
     32808-102
     32817-102
     32863-104
     32864- 93
     32873-102
     32875-103
     32898-101
     32905-103
     32946-103    1016 yds.          60       609 60
                          less 40%            243 84
                          On contract         365 76

Shipped direct              f.o.b. Veazie
  Freight prepaid,
    B/L attached
On or about January 1, 1912, our new, modern, fireproof, eight story build-
ing at the S. W. corner of Water St. and Coenties Slip will be ready.
We will occupy the entire premises, affording us much larger
      quarters and greatly increased facilities.
```

OCT 9 1911

B.N. Morris's primary canvas provider

CLARK & SMITH CO.
MAHOGANY,
FOREIGN AND DOMESTIC WOODS AND VENEERS.

TERMS 1½%-10 days   OFFICE, 231 MEDFORD STREET, CHARLESTOWN DISTRICT.

BOSTON, MASS.,   June 5, 1911

SOLD TO   Mr. B. N. Morris,

ORDER NO.   SHIPPED VIA

DESCRIPTION.	PER M.	AMOUNT.
973 feet 1" Mahogany Shorts	$ 90.00	$ 87.57

BACON & ROBINSON WOOD CO.
W. B. CROSSMAN, Manager

OFFICES: 11 BROAD ST. AND 130 FRANKLIN ST
YARD ON WASHINGTON ST.

785

BANGOR, 7-21 1911

SOLD TO B. N. Morris

July 19	Bill rendered		28 00	
	½ cd. P Hdwd		4 00	32 00
	del L. N. Jewett			
	Hay & Olive St Veazie			
	order #288			
	Please remit.			

JUL 22 1911

Palmer & Parker Co

ESTABLISHED 1833

Foreign & Domestic Cabinet Woods

HARDWOOD LUMBER
AIR DRIED AND KILN DRIED

IMPORTERS & MANUFACTURERS OF

MAHOGANY AND VENEERS

CABLE ADDRESS "MAHOGANY"
A. B. C. 5TH EDITION WESTERN UNION CODE
Telephone Connections

OFFICE: 103 MEDFORD ST., CHARLESTOWN DISTRICT

Terms 60 ds. or 2% 10 ds.   Boston   June 26, 1911.

Sold to   B. N. MORRIS,

169 pcs.	547 ft	1" A.D. Mahogany			.08½	$46.50
61 "	646 ft	1" "			.14	90.44
26 "	532 ft	1" "	"	18-22"	.17	90.44
						227.38

f.o.b. Boston

Mar 16 1912

Mr. B. N. Morris
Veazie Me

Terms   To H. N. Merrill   Dr.

Mar 16	For	5090 ft Maple Paddle Plank @ $35	178 15	
	"	1764 " Birch Boards @ 40 per M	70 56	
	"	1470 " Ash @ 25.00	36 75	
	del Veazie.			385 46

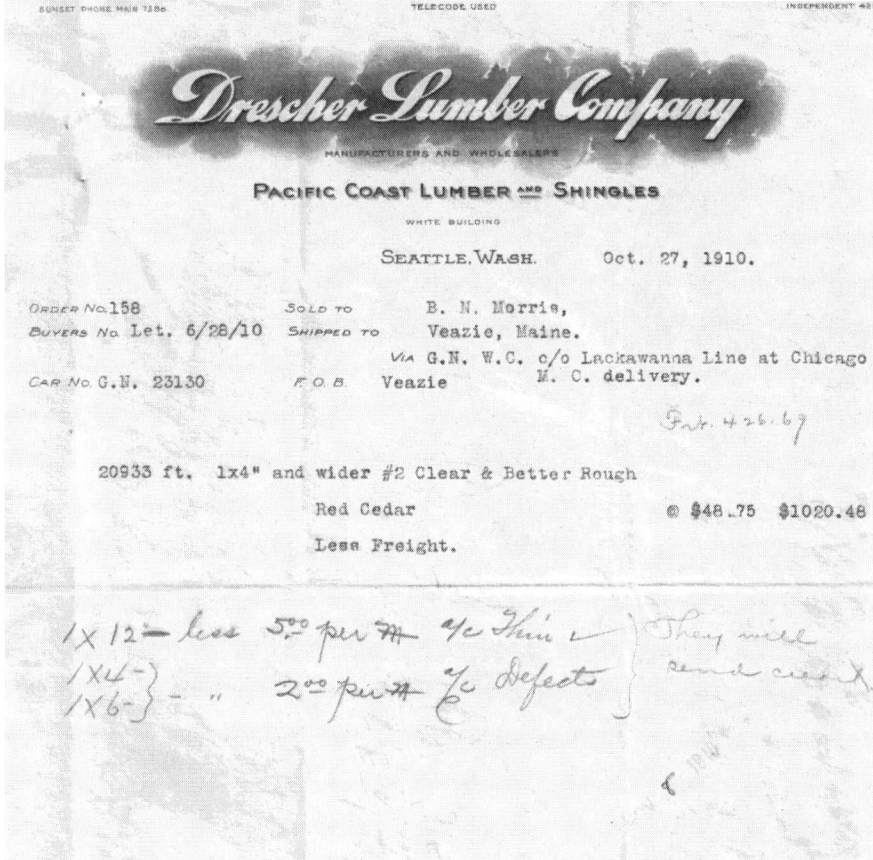

Importing Western red cedar in 1910-- Morris desires credit for defective stock

Drescher Lumber Company

MANUFACTURERS AND WHOLESALERS

PACIFIC COAST LUMBER AND SHINGLES

WHITE BUILDING

SEATTLE, WASH.   March 7, 1911.

Mr. B. N. Morris,
Veazie,
Maine.

Dear Sir:

In connection with your letter of Feb. 27th, we beg to advise, that the credit which Mr. Drescher agreed to allow you on G. N. car #23130, our invoice of Oct. 27th, 1910 is as follows:

1 x 12 - 1702 ft. @ $5.00		$8.51
Balance of car 19231 Ft. 2.00		38.46
Total credit		$46.97.

Yours truly,

DRESCHER LUMBER COMPANY,

By [signature]

WTM/LS.

P. S. --- The Mill man from the Mill from which this lumber was shipped, is in the East, and may possibly call on you, in which event, will thank you to show the stock to him.

W.T.M.

MAR 13 1911

Response to a letter of complaint

B. N. MORRIS
BUILDER OF
CANVAS CANOES
CANVAS MOTOR BOATS

OARS, PADDLES
CANOE FITTINGS

TELEGRAPH ADDRESS
VEAZIE

HULLS OR COMPLETE EQUIPMENT

CABLE ADDRESS
MORRIS, BANGOR

VEAZIE, MAINE, Jan 25" 1912

Drescher Lumber Co
Seattle, Wash.

Gentlemen;-

I have agreed to allow Mr B.N.Morris a lump sum of $40.00 on car C.M.&St P 25134 shipped August 22" 1911, on account of our shipping black colored stock, please make credit to their account on our books accordingly, they will remit for the car on this basis,

Yours very truly

Morris receives credit for defective lumber

March 23, 1912.

Mr. Geo. H. Hamlin,
Bangor, Maine.

Dear Sir;--

Yours received, enclosed find check for one hundred ($100.) dollars on account. I just noticed that you charged me $40.00 per M for that maple which is $10.00 per M more than on the other and I sorry to say the lumber is not worth as much as previous lots by $10. per M. It was sawed very poor and I guess that they put in all of the hearts by the looks of it, and I ought to have a credit of at least fifty dollars on this car.

I hope you won't think I am asking to much and it is up to you to make any allowance that you feel to, but the lumber is not worth over $35.00 per M for my use. As soon as I hear from you I will send the balance

Yours very truly,

BNM/TWN.

B. N. MORRIS.

Morris demands credit for maple that wasn't up to standard

The Morris Canoe

1911 tax bill from the Town of Veazie

Assessment regarding the connection of Charlie Morris's Flagg Street residence to the Veazie sewer system, dated January 14, 1916. Interesting that this bill is among B.N. Morris Company receipts.

Kathryn Hilliard Klos

Morris "Fun Facts"

Charles Morris was the first Veazie resident to have a telephone at his home on Flagg Street. His telephone number was "1". The Flagg Street house was the first in town to have a flush toilet. But it would seem Charlie wasn't into modern technology in every way: while Bert Morris was selling high-end automobiles in the 1920s, Charlie was using a carriage of his own making, drawn by his horse Gypsy. Charlie's canoe-- Morris 15232 (c.1917)-- a 16 foot Model A, type 1, with heart-shaped decks-- is now in the possession of his great-great-great grandson.

In an image from the 1930s, Louie King takes his dog Makela for a paddle in great-grandfather Charlie Morris's Model A type 1 Morris. Louie's grandson now has the canoe. (courtesy Louie King)

Morris 4210 was owned by Woodrow Wilson (courtesy the Florence Griswold Museum)

President Woodrow Wilson's 16 foot Morris 4510 (c.1907) resides in the Florence Griswold Museum, Old Lyme, Connecticut. The Wilson family brought the canoe to Old Lyme in 1908, when visiting a summer art colony overseen by Florence Griswold.

Environmentalist **Sigurd Olson** had two Morris canoes. His 15 foot Morris 2972 (c.1905) is part of the collection of the Minnesota Historical Society in St. Paul, and the other is at Northland College in Ashland, Wisconsin, hanging in the Sigurd Olson Environmental Institute.

Canoe builder **Joe Seliga**'s 18 foot Morris 4101 (c.1906) is a rare Model D. The Seliga family also had a 15 foot Morris, which Joe used as a basis for canoes he built from 1938 until his death in 2005.

The Morris paddled by conservationist **John Apperson**, noted for protecting the Adirondack Forest Preserve and for preservation of Lake George and its islands, is on loan to the Bolton Historical Museum in Bolton Landing, New York.

President Abraham Lincoln's son, **Robert Todd Lincoln**, owned Morris 14851-- a 17' Tuscarora, currently located at his summer home, *Hilene*, in Manchester, Vermont. This canoe is the only confirmed Tuscarora in the Morris database.

> TEN MILE RIVER
>
> There is nothing I enjoy more than canoeing, especially in spring and autumn. Rowing, swimming, fishing, and skating are all very well in their way, but give me a good canoe on a stream which has a fairly swift current. Last spring my father bought me a Morris canoe from a place near Bangor, Maine. It was shipped promptly, for I got the shipping receipt; but it was nearly two weeks in coming through to Providence. I advise people who are going to have goods come by freight to order a month early. I keep my canoe on the Ten Mile River, near Providence. I can easily ride out to the boat-house on my bicycle. The canoe is seventeen feet long and holds four people comfortably.
>
> The river, which empties into the Seekonk, is a beautiful stream. The boat-house stands on slack-water above a dam. We pass under a bridge immediately after leaving the house, and soon run up to a point where the river is not more than thirty feet wide. It is very winding, and the banks are overhung with bushes. At one point it is crossed by an old arched bridge of stone, very picturesque. After paddling up a mile or two we come to the dam at Hunt's Mills. We can carry the canoe around the dam and then go a long way farther.
>
> One day last spring the water was high, and the swift current swept me round a bend under some bushes and tipped me out. I got thoroughly drenched. Fortunately I could swim, for the water at that point was over my head. I learned to swim three summers before, but this was my first chance to swim in an emergency. The boy who was with me could not swim, but he clung to the bushes and pulled himself out on the bank.

The student essay above comes from a book of exercises in English composition by Lamont Hammond, published by Charles

Scribner's Sons in 1907. Not only does the author describe his Morris canoe, but reminds us that, early in the twentieth century, not everyone knew how to swim.

Morris placed advertising in magazines of all types, from those concerned with sporting, such as *Forest and Stream*, to magazines of general interest such as *Judge*. WCHA member Denise Card sent me the June-July 1918 issue of *American Cookery*, which seems an unlikely place to find an ad for a canoe.

In naming the Morris canoes they carried, Abercrombie & Fitch exercised a bit more imagination than A,B,C,D, or Indian, but not much imagination when it came to colors. Dan Miller shared the following:

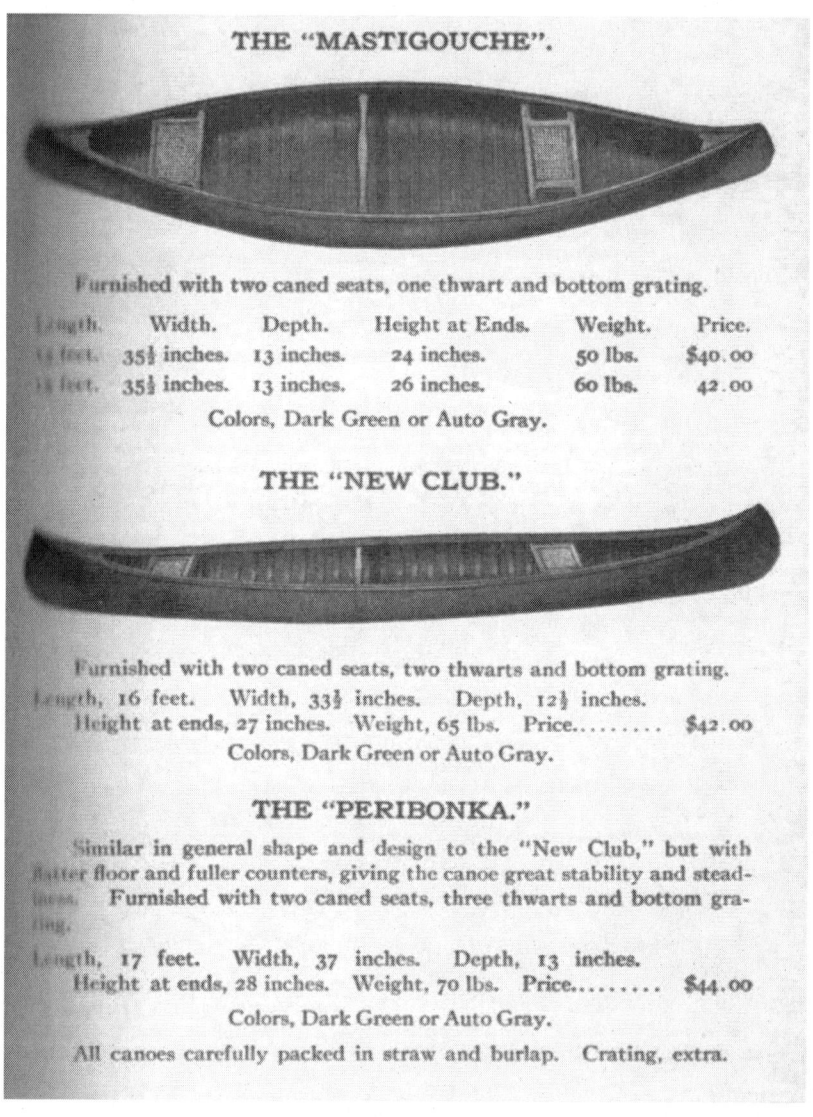

THE "MASTIGOUCHE".

Furnished with two caned seats, one thwart and bottom grating.

Length	Width	Depth	Height at Ends	Weight	Price
15 feet	35½ inches	13 inches	24 inches	50 lbs	$40.00
16 feet	35½ inches	13 inches	26 inches	60 lbs	42.00

Colors, Dark Green or Auto Gray.

THE "NEW CLUB."

Furnished with two caned seats, two thwarts and bottom grating.
Length, 16 feet. Width, 33½ inches. Depth, 12½ inches.
Height at ends, 27 inches. Weight, 65 lbs. Price......... $42.00
Colors, Dark Green or Auto Gray.

THE "PERIBONKA."

Similar in general shape and design to the "New Club," but with flatter floor and fuller counters, giving the canoe great stability and steadiness. Furnished with two caned seats, three thwarts and bottom grating.

Length, 17 feet. Width, 37 inches. Depth, 13 inches.
Height at ends, 28 inches. Weight, 70 lbs. Price......... $44.00
Colors, Dark Green or Auto Gray.
All canoes carefully packed in straw and burlap. Crating, extra.

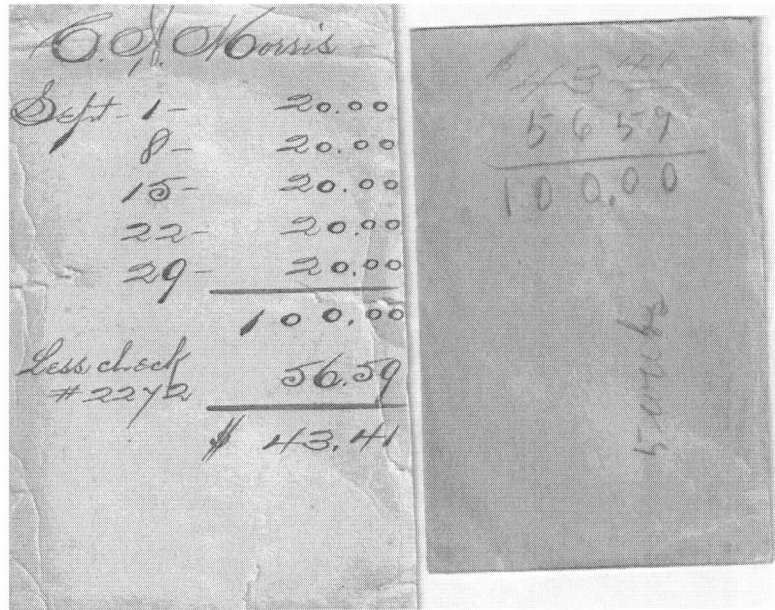

Charlie Morris's pay envelope, found in the former Morris home on Flagg Street in Veazie, likely represents income received from B.N. Morris. The early version of a pay stub on the left accompanied the 2 ½ by 4 ½ inch envelope on the right, which would have contained cash.

***

WCHA Assemblies are enormously fun…

Denis Kallery and Kathy Klos paddle Dave Winder's 13' Morris 16883 in Assembly 2011's Paddle-By and Salute (courtesy Ted Michel)

Kathy Klos on the steps of the former Morris home in Veazie with her dogs Charlie and Bert

About The Author

Kathryn Hilliard Lykken Klos was born in Minneapolis, where she grew up, married, and had a number of wonderful children. The daughter of a high school English teacher and a mom who loved to write, Kathy hopes they are smiling down on her writing endeavors.

Education-wise, Kathy attended Macalester College in St. Paul, Minnesota, focusing on literature and theater; graduated from the University of Minnesota School of Nursing with a BSN; and received a JD from William Mitchell College of Law. She has enjoyed writing all her life, has worked as a registered nurse, and has stayed out of court as much as possible.

Although a Minnesotan at heart, Kathy has lived in Michigan's Upper Peninsula since 2002, where she shares a home with beings of human, canine, feline and avian persuasions.

The Morris Canoe is Kathy's sixth published book and first attempt at non-fiction. Aside from writing, her passions include history, genealogy, Nature, animals, books, movies, making YouTube videos, and paddling wooden canoes. She has served on the board of the Wooden Canoe Heritage Association and manages Facebook pages related to the Morris and other wooden canoes.

Denis Kallery waves from the loft of his canoe shop

Happy the man, and happy he alone,
He who can call today his own:
He who, secure within, can say,
Tomorrow do thy worst, for I have lived today.
Be fair or foul or rain or shine
The joys I have possessed, in spite of fate, are mine.
Not Heaven itself upon the past has power,
But what has been, has been, and I have had my hour.
--John Dryden

The Morris Canoe

Copyright 2014, Kathryn Hilliard Klos
Cover by Margaret Marion Barnes
December 2014 Edition

The Morris Canoe

Kathryn Hilliard Klos

Made in United States
North Haven, CT
16 June 2024

53710519R00141